ODDS AGAINST SURVIVAL

'gaining insight'

Other books by Odette Marie B. K. Fischer
"Programmeur Analyste" *(DEC) (analyst programmer)*
"Technician en Informatique" *(computer technician)*
Printed in Canada 1973, 1974

ODDS AGAINST SURVIVAL

'gaining insight'

by

Odette Marie B. K. Fischer

First Edition

To protect the innocence of their families, the names herein are fictitious, and any similarity to the name, or history of any person is entirely coincidental and unintentional.

DEDICATION

To my daughter Odette Véronique, whose love and understanding kept me alive and forced me to relearn beyond all expectation

TABLE OF CONTENTS

ACKNOWLEDGMENT

The ability to write this book and the success of my recovery depended on many people that I would like to thank with all my heart. To my deceased father, Léopold Bourget, who helped me to keep my spirit inside my body. I was at a point at the base of the canyon where it would have been easier for me to die, to just let go. But Dad's spirit was there to be sure I stayed in my body and I fought back to survive.

To my mother, Juliette, for having brought me into this world. Thank you for being beside me when I awoke from my comatose period. Thank you for inviting my Canadian friends when I buried John in the family plot.

To my daughter, Odette Véronique, for getting help and saving my life, for being beside me during the sad and happy times of my recovery. I know it was very difficult for you to go through. Without you, I don't know where I would be today.

To my sisters, Élizabeth, Monique, and their husbands Gabriel Ouellet and Rodrigue Dionne for all the support and encouragement they gave me. On top of being family members, they are precious friends in my life.

I also owe tremendous thanks to my French Canadian, American, Italian, Chilean, Russian and Argentinean friends who are too numerous to mention. You were there when my spirit and body needed you. Your presence turned lights on inside my heart.

To the medical doctors and orthodontists who treated me with maximum professionalism toward my recovery: Dr. Kolar Murthy, Dr. Anthony Alter, Dr. Aimée Viroff, Dr. John Moeller, Dr. Real Potvin, Dr. Donald Hugues, Dr. Irwin Hoffman, Dr. Veena Mummaneni, Dr. Georges S. Hoffman, Dr. Bruce Becker, Dr. Andrew Matsunaga, Dr. Norman Nagel, and Dr. Scott Bennion.

I have been fortunate to work with several writers, editors, publishers, and motion picture producers who took the time to reeducate me professionally. . . Pat Miller, Marcello Danon, Dean Coffin, Maria-Estela Lorca, Caroline Hensley, Kathleen Sublette, Michelle Bourbeau, David Chambers, Eileen Allen, Danielle Smith, Tory (Victoria) Devitt Evans, Matthew R. Evans and editor-in-chief, Ellaine Greitzer.

A very special thanks to my new husband, David E. Fischer, for supporting me during my long recovery. I would also like to thank my husband for challenging my doctors and their diagnosis and qualifications while I was still in a vegetative state.

I believe that it is when you reach the bottom that you really know who your friends are. On this thought, I want to thank my French Canadian friend, Elaine Fortin whom I met in Los Angeles, California, 14 years ago. Elaine has always been there to support my daughter and me. In addition, she has been encouraging me for eight years to realize in this "second life" one of my goals . . . writing my nonfiction book. Her subsistence motivated me to complete that dream . . .

Odds Against Survival/ 'gaining insight'

I love you all, and god bless you

PREFACE

Mrs. Odette Fischer is a patient of mine who went through a series of experiences following an accident she and her husband had in the mountains of Southern California. Over the years, Odette has been coming to see me for neurological care. She had expressed quite a few experiences that she had, the majority of which were mainstream experiences, while quite a few were off beat experiences with the people she had to encounter following her accident.

Odds Against Survival/'gaining insight' is a chronology of events and also exposé of experiences that Odette had with various people she came in contact with following the accident during Christmas of 1982. She has done an exceptional job in not only categorizing the events, but keeping the chronology in mind as best as she could while limited by significant post-traumatic amnesia syndrome. This book *Odds Against Survival*/'gaining insight' is an exceptionally well written personal evaluation of many physicians and other medical personnel Odette had, fortunately or unfortunately, come in contact with.

Mrs. Odette Fischer asked me to write a preface to this book. After reading through the book, written in 19 chapters, with each chapter essentially expressing the psychosocial reaction she had with many contacts, including her family, friends, physicians, and other medical personnel, both during active hospitalization and as years went by. She essentially chronicles ten years of her life that dramatically changed following the accident. I have no doubt many of the readers will feel for the pathos this patient went through and many of the experiences may, in fact, parallel real life "out there." At times, I have shared extreme degrees of sympathy for the patients, but the fortitude she had in sitting down and putting all her emotional experiences on paper is exceptional. The book *Odds Against Survival/*'gaining insight' expounds the basic philosophy of life experiences, the shape and reshape of one's life. I acknowledge the faith that Mrs. Fischer put in me while she was my patient and in asking me to write a few words in the preface section of this book. This should make interesting and enjoyable reading to one and all who have had contact with people who have undergone a trauma and some of the trials and tribulations that patients go through afterwards. All of the personality evaluations, qualifications, and experiences are that of Mrs. Odette Fischer and reflect rather raw, heartfelt feeling. I have no reservation in recommending this book.

Sincerely yours,

Kolar N. Murthy, M.D.

FOR MY READERS

I wrote this story myself from notes I took and from what was told to me. I am French Canadian, born and raised in Québec. After my accident, I could not write English as well as before this happened. At one time I was in full command of the English language, as well as my native French.

I was a hostess for French television shows in Québec, and co-producer in Hollywood, California, for Buenos Aires, Argentina. But two days after Christmas, 1982, in the mountains of Southern California, many memories of people and words were erased. Some very beautiful things and some very dreadful things have happened since that day.

This is my story exactly as I have written it. Where my memory failed me because of my brain damage injury, it is taken from what my friends and my wonderful daughter have told me. It is written also from what I recorded everyday in seven thick notebooks.

I hope you learn something from my story; about the tremendous tasks someone who is brain injured faces to recreate their life; to be rehabilitated. You will also learn about making medical choices, about medical practice and why we must all learn to take control of our own treatment. And finally, you will see a picture of the U.S. justice system and decide whether it is safe to place our blind trust in that process. Most of all, I hope you will see faith and courage and the ability to persevere, as you join me on my long journey back to wellness in search of the person I was before.

Now, I will tell you my story.

Odette Marie

CHAPTER 1 - THE AWAKENING

Everything was warm and peaceful. Blue skies surrounded me. No more worries, no pain. Without knowing where I was, I felt comfortable and secure. No smells or sounds disturbed me. I could not feel my body. It was a tremendous feeling of joy and release. Suddenly, my deceased father, Léopold, stood next to me. He seemed to be urging me to do something. My daughter's face flashed into my mind and I knew what he was telling me. Go back and be with Véronique, she needs you very much.

It was calm, and quiet where I was and I felt joy listening to my father; but a great sense of urgency overcame me. I must go to Véronique. She needs me. I must leave this place. I have to go back . . . . nothing else matters.

In the middle of January, 1983, I awoke in a psychiatric ward of a French Hospital, l'Hôtel-Dieu de Lévis, in Québec, not knowing where I was. The walls were white and I could see blue sky through the window. Outside, a blanket of snow covered the ground. A doctor was speaking "You had an accident, Madame Kuhlman, you had an accident." But nothing registered in my mind. The only thing I wanted was to speak to my husband, John.

Alone in my room, I would grab the telephone and call my

parents-in-law in California. My mother-in-law, Lenore Kuhlman, would always tell me, "John isn't here." Then I would try again and again, because it was important that I speak to him. My mother-in-law would repeat, "Odette Marie, John isn't here. But, when he arrives, I will tell him to call you back."

I made these long distance phone calls two to three times a day from Québec to California. When my sister, Simone, was informed of these calls, she asked Dr. Compre to transfer me to a bedroom without a telephone. But it seemed as if there was no answer to my question. "Where is John? He is my husband. I need to speak to him."

I could not understand why Dr Compre, a psychiatrist, would tell me every day, "You can't speak to John. John can't call you back. You had an accident. John is dead." It didn't matter what he was telling me. At this time, my mind could not comprehend it.

Then, a few weeks later when a nurse told me, "Your husband is dead," I said, "Stop telling me that. Every day you tell me the same thing. I don't want to hear it." I became very agitated. The nurse answered, "I'll get your psychiatrist to come to see you." The fuzziness in my brain was clearing. It was the first time in a month and a half that I felt alive, my spirit was back in my body. They could tell me anything they wanted, but how could I know if it was the truth? How could I believe them?

"You wish to speak with me, Mrs. Kuhlman?" Dr. Compre asked as he came into my room.

"Dr. Compre, would you ask your nurse to stop telling me that John is dead? I know you say he is dead. But you can say what you want, until I see John's body, I won't believe you."

"Madame Kuhlman, for many weeks I have waited for your brain to register that John is dead. But, this is the first morning that you and I can talk about it. Your brain is finally registering what I wanted you to understand."

"How did I get here . . . to this hospital?"
I needed to know what I was doing in this French hospital.

Dr. Compre explained to me. "In December, you had an accident in California. Your parents-in-law called your family here in Québec to make them aware of your serious condition. Some members of your family did go to Los Angeles to see you. Then later you were transferred here."

"If John is dead like you say, where is he?"

"John's body is at the mortuary in Los Angeles."

"If what you say is true, did he suffer?"

"He didn't have time to suffer. He broke his neck. He died instantly."

I asked why I didn't remember anything. The psychiatrist answered, "Madame Kuhlman, you have been comatose for over six weeks with a brain injury. Much memory has been erased."

After my discussion with the nurse in the early morning, and now with Dr. Compre, I still felt a need to check with someone else. What was the truth? I called my old friend, Dustin, who oversaw my business affairs at his home in Ontario, Canada. He had been calling me every day since I woke up in the French hospital and we spoke briefly. But he never disclosed to me the story about John. I told Dustin what I learned and asked if it was true.

"Yes Odette Marie. You and John had an accident in the mountains in California. John died there."

"How do you know it is true?" I asked. "You didn't see John dead."

"I didn't see John's body, but the accident was on television and John's parents called us. We know it's true. His body is being kept frozen until you can identify him."

"Will you come with me to see John? I must see him. This is the only way that I'll believe it. I want to touch John."

My friend told me, "When you go back to California, I'll go with you. We'll ask your parents-in-law the name of the mortuary where John is and we'll go there together."

After talking with Dustin, I felt a little bit relieved. I wasn't going to be alone when I would be released from l'Hôtel Dieu de Lévis, the hospital where they had taken me from California.

Every day, my sister Cécile would bring my seven-year-old daughter to the hospital. It was a joy to see Véronique and hug her. One time she told me, "Mama, today I learned at Cécile's restaurant how to make pizza. Tomorrow, I'll bring you some." She was not crazy about her school work because she was forced to go to a French school where everything was taught in French. It was difficult for her after living in California for six years.

On many visits, Véronique would say, "Mom, I saved your life. It is because of me that you are here." I told Véronique how lucky I was to have a child like her. Since the accident I wanted to live just to raise her and see her children, and be able to learn exactly how she saved my life. I wanted to remember that and someday tell her children about it.

Another sister, Simone, would call me every day asking, "Who is with you? Are Cécile and René (brother/sister) coming there to see you?" She told me that when they were in Los Angeles, Cécile and René stole a lot of my personal property. She also told me that Corky, my brother-in-law, didn't care if I died and that my mother-in-law blamed me because John was dead.

Simone's bitterness could destroy one person after another. I let her talk and then hung up the telephone. My heart was very heavy.

The next morning, when I saw Dr. Compre, I told him what Simone had said when she called from Montréal.

"I don't know why Simone says such things, trying to destroy my brother, René, my sister, Cécile, and the Kuhlman family."

"I don't know either," Dr. Compre said, "but don't worry about her. You have to concentrate on getting better. If she calls again, don't talk to her."

From that time on, I never did.

CHAPTER 2 - ACCIDENT

Many times, I would ask God why I woke up in the psychiatric ward of a French hospital. I couldn't remember anything about what happened. But day by day, with the help of my daughter, I slowly began to learn about the accident. Véronique became my memory. Later, I learned the truth from hospital employees, psychiatrists, newspaper stories, and from my friends. I made notes on everything.

John's mother told me that although her son and I were separated for a while, we were still a family. I could remember nothing.

Apparently (according to what I was told), I had called the Kuhlman family on Christmas Day 1982 before the accident to wish them a Merry Christmas and I also spoke with John. He told me that he was very sad over our separation. We loved each other, even though for a while it was good for us to be living apart. John wanted Véronique and me to go with him to see the snow in the mountains on December 27th. He knew how much I loved to see snow and how it reminded me of my home in Québec. We planned on going for a drive in the San Gabriel mountains, north of Los Angeles, two days after Christmas.

Véronique told me this after I was released from the hospital. By now, I could understand and comprehend enough to make notes.

On December 26th, I was making dinner for some friends when I had to run across the street to a neighbor to get my daughter. My daughter's two-year-old dog, Boomer, ran into the street in front of me. He was hit by a car. I left Véronique home with friends and took him to a veterinary hospital where they put a splint on his broken leg and kept him overnight.

The next morning, we went to pick up Boomer at the hospital and then went to get Daddy, as Véronique calls him, at his apartment. It was eight o'clock in the morning. John was sad to see Boomer with his leg in a cast, but was very happy to see us. Véronique continued to tell me what she remembered.

> *"Daddy drove us up into the mountains, and at one place he saw a spot to park. We all got out of the car. Boomer kept falling down with his broken leg. He couldn't stay on his legs, Mom. So Daddy asked you if at the next stop, you could stay in the car with Boomer because he did not want the dog to get hurt more. You and Boomer went back in the car to wait for Daddy and me.*
>
> *Shortly after we were all back in the car driving on Angeles Crest Highway, Daddy saw a nice clean area at a turn out where we could stop and admire the snow and the canyon. He said, 'Odette Marie, please stay in the car with Boomer. I will go with Véronique outside so we can touch the snow. Daddy and I went walking on the snow. Suddenly, he disappeared through the snow. He was gone. I rushed back to the car shouting, Daddy is dead! He fell down the canyon. You screamed at me,'What? Where is Daddy?'*

'He is down the canyon. I think he is dead. He disappeared in the snow.'

You told me, 'Stay in the car with Boomer. Mama is
going to try to help Daddy. I want to save Daddy's life.'

Mama, don't go. You will die too.

'Mama will be right back. I'm just going to find Daddy,
and help him.' (I couldn't let him die). 'Véronique, stay with
Boomer in the car and lock the doors. I'll be right back.
Don't go out of the car for any reason.'

(According to my daughter, I went to the middle of the
turnaround place, where the snow was stacked.) "Mom, I
could see you walking and you disappeared just like
Daddy.

I cried very loud. I was screaming for you and Daddy
for a long time, but I did not open the car door. I stayed
in the car like you told me to do before you left. There were
two men who came first. They drove up and stopped. They
asked me where you were. I told them you were down there.
Both men went in the middle of the highway to stop another
car. The car they stopped had a lady and a man in it. The
lady got out of her car, came up to me and tried to talk
through the closed window to find out what happened. I
was still screaming. The lady stayed there to help me.
The two other men were looking for you down the canyon,
shouting that everything was going to be fine and they
were going to get help for you. The lady asked me to open
the door because she was going to help Boomer and me.
She sat with me in our car and her boyfriend went to find
help. When the lady's boyfriend came back, he said that
there was another accident and the rescue team was trying

to help other people in a different part of the mountain. After a long time, they finally came.

Boomer barked at everybody. He was barking and growling. When the policeman came, he asked me questions. After that, another policeman, a Sheriff, got in the car, or tried to. He asked me to move Boomer before Boomer bit him.

During the time the Sheriff was asking me questions about who you where and what Daddy's name was, two helicopters were both searching for you and Daddy. They saw you, Mom. They were flying around until the rescue team was pulling you up with ropes. Some rescue men went down with a big red thing to carry you out. One helicopter kept looking for Daddy. Then they put you in the helicopter very fast and the helicopter went away. They would not let me see you. I was still in the car with the lady, wanting to get out. The Sheriff told me that the rescue team and the helicopter were going to continue looking for Daddy until they'd found him. But, in the meantime, the police drove Boomer and me to the police station."

That was my darling daughter's memory of everything that happened. I took it from the notes I made while I was recovering and afterward when I was released from the French hospital.

I do remember feeling conscious during the complete period of time that I fell 600 feet to the middle of the canyon. My arms were holding my head. I never let my feet touch the ground. I knew that I couldn't walk because I had so much pain. I remember seeing a huge tree, the tree that saved my life by breaking my fall. But I was in tremendous pain and could not think about saving John anymore. I wished my spirit would leave my body. I was scared, but I felt that this huge tree held powers and was revealing to me what my Dad wanted for me, my security.

At times, I could see my father, who had died two years before. I was able to hear his voice. He wouldn't allow me to let my spirit separate from my body. Dad was telling me to stay alive. He kept my spirit and my body together.

Dad and I had such a long talk there. He had the power to make me remember about Véronique and Boomer in the car, waiting for me to come back. That's when I started to be afraid to die.

I asked God to keep me with my daughter, Véronique. I was hurting everywhere in my body, but I prayed to stay alive to raise my daughter and be able to see her children. I was so afraid to die, I couldn't accept death.

I bargained with God. "I don't mind not being able to walk anymore and work. I'm not asking you that. I just want to be with my daughter, I need to be with her."

There was a report made by the Deputy Sheriff who managed the entire rescue operation. The following account of the accident is from a taping made by Sergeant John Shaughnessy, a thirty-year veteran of the Crescenta Valley Sheriff's Station of the Los Angeles County Sheriff's Department.

"It was a bright, beautiful day in the San Gabriel mountains. A lot of snow had fallen for several days, but that day was clear and very cold. The sun would melt some of the snow on the surface, so water would form on top of the snow, then freeze as each day got colder. That's what caused your husband and you to slip from where you were. There had been a buildup of ice for several days.

Your husband was driving slowly up the mountain along

Angeles Crest Drive. Your car was followed by another car with two young men in it. Your husband pulled off the road into a turn-about at the side of the road to let the two young men pass, a courtesy they appreciated. Your car continued for a while to another turn-about, where it pulled off the road again. To clear the road on previous days, the plow and the snow blower had deposited a wall of snow at the canyon edge of the turn-about where you stopped. It was a wall, four or five feet high, maybe more, melting and freezing. The ice was so thick, a man's weight couldn't have broken through it. The top of the wall was flat and looked level, but it wasn't. It sloped down toward the canyon, the higher side of its slope being closer to the road. Your daughter told us -- and that little girl is very intelligent and very lovely -- your seven- year-old daughter told us that your husband climbed up on top of the supposedly level, and flat wall of snow. It was like a platform for him.

Apparently he dropped something near his feet, bent over to pick it up and started sliding off the ice platform into the valley or canyon below. The mountain slopes down steeply from there, at an angle of forty-five, maybe up to sixty degrees, so he slid very fast, head first, and there was nothing to stop him. He went out of sight. When you came over to the wall of snow to try to rescue Mr. Kuhlman, you made the same mistake, but slid in a slightly different direction. You were stopped by a big pine tree, where the rescue team found you.

There are five mountain rescue teams. All are volunteer snow and mountains lovers who get paid one dollar a year for their work. They come to training meetings every month and frequently go out into the mountains for practice rescues. One man will be elected to 'get lost' and the others will have to find him. All five Sheriff rescue teams participate in these exercises.

Each team has a four-wheel drive truck with a strong A-frame mounted in front with a long steel cable running through it. The cable is wound on a big spool and can be let out many hundreds of feet and rewound again, all by power from the truck. The four men in the crew of each team have steel spikes they strap on to their feet like claws for climbing on snowy slopes. There are long ropes, also extending from the A-frame, the men hold onto when 'walking' down or up the side of a mountain. Two of the four men in the crew are paramedics; they carry medical supplies on their backs. They also have a litter, a stretcher with sides to keep the victim from rolling. The litter carries a backboard to which the victim is strapped to prevent any further injury to the spine. There's a neck collar to fasten around the victim's neck to keep the head from rolling and keep the vertebrae in place. Those people, and that equipment, arrived at your accident site within forty minutes of receiving the call. The call, by the way, came from a lady who was stopped in her car by the two young men and told to call for help. You see, the young men, after passing your car, went on for a ways, then returned down the road. When they reached you car, all they saw was your daughter in the car, calling out. They went on for a short distance, stopped at another turn-about and looked back at your car and your daughter. They decided something was wrong and came back. That's when they stopped the lady and told her to call for help. (The real accolades for your rescue go to them.)

The rescue team went over the crest and walked down the mountainside on their spikes, holding onto the ropes. They found you by the big tree and began giving you an intravenous solution and preparing to lift you on the backboard into the litter. You were probably unconscious, but you were muttering something very softly in strange words they couldn't understand. By this time, a second Search and Rescue Team had arrived at the site to help. While the paramedics were preparing you, one of the Sheriff's converted army helicopters arrived to start searching from the air. They saw that the paramedics had found you, and so they landed on the roadway near your car. The truck's power pulled on the cable, and you came up in the litter, guided by the men from the rescue teams. You were carried to the helicopter and at about 4:30p.m., were on your way to the hospital. After these operations, the second Search and Rescue team that had arrived started to search for your husband. A second Sheriff's helicopter arrived and began to search for your husband further down the valley. Of course, we were all in touch with each other by radio. The Search and Rescue teams and the helicopter worked a long time on finding your husband. When the ground rescue teams became exhausted, another team arrived and worked on the mountainside until about 3:30 in the morning. The second helicopter abandoned the search after dark, returning the next morning to continue operations. Eventually, they found your husband about 1200 feet down the moun-

tainside.

As you know, he was dead and probably died instantly when his head caught a hole in the icy mountain, breaking his neck. I should say, too, that the afternoon we brought you to the hospital, we took your daughter to our Sheriff's station, gave her something to eat, and talked with her further. You have a very bright and lovely daughter. She gave us the name of her Uncle Corky, whom we called. Inasmuch as he was part of your family, we released Véronique and Boomer to Corky Kuhlman, which California law indicates is the right thing to do in such a case.

But, some time later, perhaps several days, I had an angry visit from your sister, Simone, objecting to our releasing your daughter to her uncle and wanting us to reverse our release. She was very upset. I explained that if we couldn't release your daughter to a member of the family, we would have to release her to Probate Court, which would have placed her in Juvenile Hall until a Probate Judge could hear the matter and decide what to do. That would have been the wrong way to handle the problem. But your sister was very unreasonable. She called later in an angry mood and mentioned that there was a lot of money involved and there would be a big fight about it. I, of course, knew nothing about that, but was very irritated and I still refused to do anything about our custody decision for Véronique."

I didn't get that taped report from the man who managed the entire rescue operation until eight years later. When I was rescued, I didn't even know that my husband was dead at thirty-eight years of age. I don't remember anything about the hospital where they took me. What was done to me? What did I eat? How did I go to the bathroom? Did my family in Québec come to California? Did my family-in-law come to see me? I didn't know anything at all and I stayed that way until six weeks later when I woke up in a hospital in Québec where my family had arranged to send me. Not to a general hospital in the city, but to a mental hospital in Lévis, a suburb of Québec. I wondered why they did that. Later on, I would find out.

CHAPTER 3 - MY FAMILY

Quite a few weeks after I regained consciousness in Québec and learned what happened, I discovered many things about my family's actions in Los Angeles. It's important to keep in mind the members of my family, especially those who had much to do with my life after the fall.

When a person is lying unconscious in a hospital after an accident such as mine, many decisions are made by the family. I could never have guessed, however, what the members of my family would decide and what actions they would take concerning me while I was comatose in the Intensive Care unit. Because much of this story deals with nine people, I will introduce them for clarification.

We were a family of seven children (Cécile, Simone, Steven, René, Sylvie, Ruth, and myself (the author), and our natural parents, Léopold and Juliette Bourget, living in Lévis, which is a Québec city suburb community across the St. Lawrence River.

The one person in my family who couldn't be in Los Angeles, but helped me very much, was my father, Léopold. We were always very close and understood each other. I have mentioned how I could see and hear him while I was lying six hundred feet down the mountainside, even though he had died two years before. He kept my spirit with my body, in spite of my terrible pain. He had the power to make me remember Véronique and Boomer in the car waiting for me. I was filled with fear and prayed not to die.

Father was a modestly successful owner of beauty shops in Québec for a period of thirty-five years. He was a tall, slender man, a gentleman, with lovely watchful blue eyes and frequently a shy, sympathetic smile. He provided generously for us until he became mentally ill and was hospitalized. I never did quite understand what his ailment was because we were all young when this happened.

One weekend he decided to take off to attend a Roman Catholic retreat. Because he was a very sensitive man and because he talked with an extremely severe Catholic priest at the retreat, he suffered great feelings of guilt. These feelings led him to a nervous breakdown and he was hospitalized for three months at St. Michel Archange Hospital.

Later, father came out of the hospital and went to work for the provincial government in Québec city. He worked there for eighteen years, even though one week a month his character seemed electrified by the moon when his behavior became bizarre. He was depressed, cried a lot, and his physical actions were sometimes violent. We never knew what he was going to do, if he was going to hurt himself or someone else. We could see his spells come on just by the look on his face. (On many occasions, my mother said that she was blamed for Dad's condition.) When it reached the point that my mother felt she couldn't handle his condition anymore, she organized a family meeting for father to be rehospitalized. In Québec, a family meeting is the final authority needed to commit a family member to a mental hospital and to control that person's life and assets. When this took place at my parent's home, we were all adults. Nevertheless, he was a lovely man and respected by everyone in the area.

Sadly, on the day of the family meeting, the entire family had the power to vote and decide if father was going to stay free or be sent back to a psychiatric ward. I don't know if I was the only one that voted against father being sent back to the psychiatric hospital, but mother got enough votes to send him back. Much later, after his release, he went back to work for the government until he retired at the age of sixty-five years.

I can now remember that during these years, I saw my father walking in the kitchen many times, his hand held close to his chest. He would say, "I have so much chest pain, mom. I have chest pain." Mother would tell him that he just liked to complain, and if the pain was so bad, he should see a doctor.

In January of 1980, Father went to see Dr. Powers in Lévis who performed several tests. He called both my parents back to a meeting at the hospital and informed them, sadly, that Dad had lung cancer. It was too advanced to perform surgery and the doctor advised my father that even radiation would not help. It was too late. Dad was treated with pain medication for about a month and finally died in February of 1980, six months after his retirement.

When I first awoke from my coma, I remembered my mother as she had been thirty years in the past. She was short and slim, with beautiful dark brown short hair, and wide brown eyes. I did not realize that this was a childhood memory. My mother is a harsh and demanding woman with strong and frequently irritating prejudices which were often expressed in her feelings about her seven children. Her manner toward some of us was frequently offensive. Mother always split her responses to the children between the Bourget (fraternal) or the Bégin (maternal) characteristics in appearance and personalities.

She knew how to be endearing to people outside of the family, making jokes and laughing, showing a happy nature. She managed to find time to help our neighbors, even though she was very busy working at home and visiting Dad at the hospital. She knew how to make people like her. On the other hand, she was unable to communicate and share warmth with some of her children. Even if we tried hard to get to know her, she always put up a facade to block us. She showed herself as a strong, capable person without any human frailties.

When people from the outside would visit us, Mother showed her relaxed nature. It was something we saw only on rare occasion because she would ask us to leave when she spoke intimately about her feelings with friends. Even though Father was ill when we were growing up, Mother had no serious problems raising her seven children. Most of us started working very young and helped her financially as best we could. I felt my mother could never accept each of her children just as they were. She favored Simone, Steven and Sylvie, always finding money to spend on them while ignoring her other children. It was a great injustice.

I remember one thing that my mother and I enjoyed together. While she would be resting on her bed, I would play the piano. We would sing together. Mother loved singing and music. She told me many times how she loved it when we sang together. It was her only way to connect with me.

Three of my sisters, Cécile, Simone, and Sylvie, and a brother, René, grew up with Bégin traits; sharp-tempered, commanding, consistently selfishly motivated and even greedy. The brother in that Bégin quartet, René, had softened somewhat in recent years, although at the time of my accident he was as greedy and unethical as our sisters Cécile, Simone and Sylvie.

My sisters Cécile, Simone and Sylvie look and think like mother. In appearance and spirit, Ruth and I are more like my father's side of the family (Bourget). My brother, René's, appearance is like the Bourget side of the family, but his character is more like mother's side. They acted toward us as if nobody on earth was better than they were and took control of everything we encountered together. It seemed that being in control was a goal for them and my mother. Nothing they could say or do was wrong in mother's eyes.

Another brother, Steven, looks like the Bégin side of the family, but takes after my father's likeness in personality and value, much like my darling Ruth and I. We can smile and laugh together as friends as well as having brother and sister loyalties. In my father's tradition we are friendly and sentimental people, as well as being warmly affectionate toward each other. In appearance we take after my father's slender build rather than the heavier, thick frame those on my mother's side have developed.

Upon awakening from a coma with brain damage, I found myself at the same hospital where father used to be. The same tactic used to commit my father to a mental hospital, a meeting of all family members, was discussed regarding me in my helpless condition. However, my brother, René, unquestionably refused to organize a family meeting to commit me after I awoke and refused to let any one of them adopt my daughter. One of my sisters, Cécile, had charged that because of my brain damage I was mentally unstable.

I was never really close to my mother. She did not try to

understand me very well. In her eyes I seemed to be someone who should do all the chores; do this, do that, wash this, sweep there. My sister, Simone, never did any of these jobs, but told mother to pass them off to me. I was the *Cinderella* in the family.

As I grew, my family life continued to be unhappy, mother constantly unwilling or unable to give me the warm and loving spirit a growing girl needs. Instead, I was given responsibility for most of the housework while my sister, Simone, was excused by mother from many chores that should have been hers.

There were many ways in which my mother and the Bégin-type children made family life unpleasant. But, in spite of these frictions, and my dear father's illnesses, I was able to find inspiration and beauty away from my family. At first I found these values in music lessons and dance training. By nine years of age I could read music and compose. At thirteen I was learning to model young people's clothing professionally. By fifteen I had progressed to high fashion modeling, presenting new styles to buyers of women's wear. After that I was modeling new creations at special events. Subsequently, I taught other girls the techniques of the professional model: posture, grace, personality, motivation and especially how to work with photographers and production people.

From modeling it was a logical advancement into working occasionally before television cameras.

About the time that I was sixteen I met a man who later in my life would provide the affectionate support I couldn't always find in my family except for my darling, and ailing father, and the other two Bourget-type children, Steven and Ruth. This man was Dustin. He was a student of classics at Sainte-Anne de la Pocatière Collège in the Kamouraska area. We became friends instantly and, on the first day we met, exchanged many words and feelings about life.

Dustin became my true friend and confidant. Unfortunately, two years went by in which I lost contact with him.

During those years, I left home and moved to a small apartment, so small there was no bedroom. It was all I could afford. I slept on the couch, trying to discover a way to find the independence my spirit needed. Trying to satisfy my business mind, and support myself with various jobs although I was only eighteen years of age. I had left a home of many quarrels.

In 1966, I graduated from l'Institut de Data Processing de Québec. Following my graduation, I started to work for the Art Engineer Co. I then founded a private college, *Institut Professionnal de Mécanographie,* which was recognized by the ministere of education. I developed the program, gave many seminars, and according to Mr. Edmund, the private education director from the Ministere of Education, I became the youngest director of a private college in the province of Québec.

That same year, I enrolled at Laval University in computer science programming courses. It was wonderful for me because Dustin was enrolled in the same courses. During our attendance he and I became close friends again, dining, studying, and just being together as often as possible. We called each other by telephone daily. Helping each other was for both of us a way of surviving. Though we were not lovers, there were no barriers between us. Our friendship was affectionate, but always platonic.

Dustin came to my apartment every weekend. I introduced him to a number of my girlfriends hoping he would find one he could love. But none of the girls appealed to him. Instead, on many evenings at my little apartment, we sang together a great variety of songs. We played poker with our friends, sometimes until very early in the morning. On those occasions Dustin made his bed on the floor in the kitchen while I slept on the sofa. On other occasions, especially on Saturday nights, we would cross the St. Lawrence River by ferry to Québec to enjoy the music and singing of a good friend, Pierre Roche, at l'Auberge des Gouverneurs, an upscale night club. We had many happy times together sharing our problems and pleasures.

At one point, I thought Dustin might like to meet my sister, Sylvie, one of the Bégin side of our family. She was young and attractive and did appeal to him. They sat up all night in the kitchen, talking. Fifteen months later he married Sylvie, and joined our family.

Before their marriage Dustin and I continued to enjoy each other's company, talking, singing and laughing together. It was a deep and lasting friendship, but I wasn't able to enjoy his company as often after the marriage because they moved to Ottawa, about three hundred miles away.

When I started my company, *Institut Professional de Mécanographie,* it was also the beginning of my *talk show* that was viewed in the province of Québec. I knew that my future life work would be in computer science, and being on the air. Later, because of its growth, IPM became incorporated under the name Institut Professionnel d'Informatique, Inc., and I founded a second company, Service Professional d'Informatique, Inc., to supply programming services to corporations needing assistance with their computer work. This was profitable and required other people to be on the payroll. It was to Dustin I turned for help in running my expanding business affairs. For years he held Power of Attorney to handle financial matters for me.

CHAPTER 4 - JOHN

Véronique's father and my husband, John, had always been fascinated by the mountains. He started climbing when he was eighteen years old. When he was young, friends had invited him to go with them one weekend, and the mountains became for him an escape from emotional stress. He used to tell me, "I can go into the mountains for three to four days, just climb and forget all my problems. I enjoy nature, I don't have to face anybody there."

For the last four years of his life, he was a member of the Sierra Club. He found happiness just seeing the beautiful trees. Natural settings and the beauty of nature became his major interest in life. He spent many vacations in the mountains, visiting all the ranges in Southern California.

At home, two rooms were filled with maps of the mountains he had walked in and climbed. The walls were covered with these maps. On each one, he marked all the paths he had followed in red pencil. I'm certain that he never dreamed he would find death in his beloved mountains.

Whenever we spoke of the potential danger of climbing, John told Véronique and me, "Mountains are places for me to relax, to see animals, and to be myself. I'll never die there."

I loved John very much, and a long time after I awoke from the coma, I started to remember our life together. We met in 1970 in Québec City, where he worked as an electronic engineer on the installation of a computer system at the Grand Theater. I was in a piano bar with a girlfriend, Johé, when a tall, elegant gentlemen with curly brown hair walked over to the piano. He stood near the pianist with a drink in his hand and adjusted his glasses, looking toward us.

Then this handsome stranger approached me and asked, "Voulez-vous danser?"
"Oui." I answered.

We giggled when we tried to communicate, but couldn't. We spent the evening together, dancing. John was unable to speak French and I was unable to speak English. After a few weekend get togethers, we did better because John bought a French-English dictionary and I began taking English courses at Berlitz school.

In July 1971, we got married. Because of John's work as an engineer, we came to live in Los Angeles. I was very much in love with my husband, but I was lonely in Los Angeles. Because I could not communicate easily with most of the people in English, I didn't have many friends there. That was due to my French accent. In Québec, I had started two data processing institutes and one data processing service company before I met John. These had been managed by a business associate during the first two years of our marriage. During that time, I took an advanced computer course at Computer Machinery Corporation. Because I continued to feel lonely, my husband finally said, "If you want, we can move back to Québec. This way, you will have your computer science business and all your friends." So, we went back to Québec where my friends and family live. We were very happy there and both of us worked for my companies.

A year after moving to Québec City, I discussed adopting a child with John. I had learned that I could not become pregnant, but I wanted to be a mother. It took us six months until we received a little Korean baby girl, born in Seoul, for adoption. She was five months old when she arrived in Québec. I was the happiest woman in the world. Being a mother and having a loving husband was everything that I could ask for.

I could not remember any of my past with John until the second year after the fall. There was so much that my brain could not comprehend but finally much of the past was coming back. I began to relive all the times John and I had spent together.

I remembered that the same week our daughter arrived at our home, John began to feel sick. He went to see a doctor and took tests, but his physician didn't know what made him feel so tired, and what caused his upset stomach. Medication was prescribed, but nothing helped. As his illness grew progressively worse, John took one month off work, stayed in bed, and worried; about what, I never knew.

When Christmas arrived that year, we thought that if we went to Los Angeles with our new little baby girl, whom we had baptized Odette Véronique, it would be good for John. His parents would love to see their first grandchild. We flew to Los Angeles and stayed with my parents-in-law for two weeks. John was still sick, running to the bathroom all the time.

His parents and I thought that maybe being a new father was making him nervous, and he needed to be alone with me for a while. So, John's parents babysat Véronique while John and I flew to Honolulu for a vacation. During our time on the Island, John looked more relaxed, but he still suffered from diarrhea, and was passing blood from his rectum.

Two weeks later, we picked up our daughter in Los Angeles and returned home to Québec. John got a second medical opinion at the Jeffrey Hale Hospital. After being examined and undergoing testing, the doctor gave us his diagnosis: John was suffering from ulcerative colitis. He would be obliged to take medication permanently.

After the diagnosis, John went to work for two afternoons a week at the office. We hired a nanny, Mrs. Morin, to take care of Véronique and John while I went back to work full time. I struggled to figure out what I could do to make John feel better. He appeared to have no idea what was troubling him, and I was also in the dark.

I retired from my talk show on computer science and sold the office building. We packed up our things and moved to Palos Verdes, California, for my husband's health. I had been on the air for eight years and would miss talking with the public who called in with questions about computer science. The show had been aired on every television station in Québec and many people signed up for the private college I had founded. But John's doctor told us that living in cold weather was bad for his health and advised us to move back to California.

As you can see, our time in Québec as a family was very short. My family and friends didn't have the chance to see our little baby grow up to be a lovely little girl. However, I had found my greatest happiness in her life. I knew only one thing, I was now a mother. My professional life was not going to take me away from my child. I wanted to raise my daughter, to share with her what I felt I never received from my own mom; love, communication, and affection. The time had arrived in my life when I needed to take flight, and try my own wings. I wanted to succeed as a mother.

After arriving in Los Angeles, John went to work as an engineer, but continued to be sick. The physician in Los Angeles who treated John told him that he was afraid that he might have colon cancer. Even though with time we found out it was not cancer, John came to blame our daughter, Véronique, for his sickness.

Before Véronique came into our life, I had only John to spoil. In my business life, he was the center of attention because he was an American living in Québec. I had 72 employees, mostly female, who spent time teaching John French. He was very attractive and received a lot of attention. But in our private lives, it was a different story. He resented Véronique for taking my time. His role had changed and he had become a father. It was his turn to give love and share his life.

One evening, after the baby was in bed, John and I played backgammon. We sat on our bed in the master bedroom and John kept getting up to run to the bathroom.

"What's wrong," I asked. "Why are you going to the bathroom so often?"

He didn't answer. He finally came back to continue our game, but had to leave again after a short time. Not realizing how he felt, I began to tease.

"If you don't stop going to the toilette so much, you'll lose the game," I laughed. John picked up the backgammon game and threw it at me. I jumped up.

"Why are you acting this way?"

"I can't concentrate, I'm running to the bathroom all the time," he said.

"It isn't normal for a man in his 30s to suffer so from colitis," I said. "You should get another medical opinion."

"I was never sick before we adopted Véronique," John said.

"She had nothing to do with what you are suffering from," I told him.

He went on like this blaming our new baby for his colitis for a long time. Could it be his illness was attention-seeking, a form of jealousy?

CHAPTER 5 - SUPPORT

John's family, his mother Lenore, his father Bud, and Corky, John's brother, lived in Los Angeles. They were the first in the family to know the facts of the accident. In April 1983, my mother-in-law informed me that because I was in the coma and seriously injured at the time of the accident, the doctor in Intensive Care asked my parents-in-law if my own parents had been informed. Lenore reported that my mother had been notified and was flying to Los Angeles with my family as soon as possible. They were aware of my condition.

Lenore told me that my mother came from Québec to Los Angeles with two of my sisters, Simone and Cécile. However, I don't recall ever seeing them or anybody else when I was at Kyung Ok Hospital. I have no recollection at all. My body was there, but my spirit was gone. If I had died at that time, it would have been okay. I could only remember the paralyzing fear I had when I was lying in the middle of the canyon. It seemed that nothing compared to the fear that I was going to die. When mother came to Los Angeles with my two sisters, they stayed in a hotel near the hospital. I was also told that my parents-in-law and Véronique came to see me every day in the hospital.

The first day that mom and my sisters saw the Kuhlmans at the hospital, they were nice to them. The second day when my parents-in-law showed up at Intensive Care, my sister, Simone, accused my mother-in-law of stealing my wedding ring, and asked where John's wedding ring was. Lenore Kuhlman told Simone, "I don't know where the rings are." Next, Simone wanted to know where my car was. Lenore informed her that the car was at her home, because the police released the car to the Kuhlmans on December 27th.

The same day, discussion of Véronique's custody also took place. Simone told Lenore that she wanted to have Véronique. My mother-in-law said something like this: "We have had Véronique since the day of the accident. The people gave custody to Corky, her uncle. We're taking good care of her, she's going to school in San Pedro. Dr. Bower, who is Corky's father-in-law, is a member of the staff at San Pedro Hospital. He'll communicate with Odette Marie's doctor to see if she can be transferred to the San Pedro Hospital. This way, Véronique will be able to see her mother every day without us having to drive on the freeway. Doctor Bower will take good care of Odette Marie."

Simone began yelling at my mother-in-law. She created such a disruption that a nurse was forced to call the hospital guard who asked my family to leave.

My mother-in-law, Lenore, said to me, "We were in deep mourning and shocked at the loss of our son. We didn't need Simone to scream at us."

In addition, Lenore disclosed to me, "I had your address book. With it I was trying to notify everybody about the accident, but Simone wanted the address book. I didn't want to give it to her. This is also why she freaked out. She kept calling at my residence every day to threaten me."

The accident had been reported in the media, so my friends knew of what had happened right away. Two of them, after talking with my mother-in-law, decided to come to see me at the hospital. They met my mother and Simone while visiting me.

Simone asked one of my friends, Marilyn, for the directions to my house. I was living in Thousand Oaks, near Marilyn's home. She gave Simone the directions. Marilyn and my other girlfriend, Indiente, also gave my sister their telephone numbers.

The next morning, Simone and mother drove to my home. Simone had called Indiente to ask if she could join my mother and her at my home and she agreed. The purpose of that visit was for my sister, Simone, to find out where my jewelry, John's ring, and my money were kept.

When Indiente learned that Simone was looking for my jewelry and other things, she said innocently, "Last week, Odette Marie showed me where she hides her jewelry and important papers. Let me show you where they are."

Once Simone discovered what she wanted, she took with her the jewelry case, and every Certificate of Deposit (CD) that I had. In addition, she asked Indiente the name of a good attorney to find out what she could do to get custody of Véronique. Again, my girl-friend told her, "I know Odette Marie's lawyer. I can give you his name."

Simone took his name and telephone number and made an appointment with my attorney, Mr. Koosch. He informed her that because I outlived my husband, I had custody of my daughter. Simone then inquired about John's life insurance policy. Mr. Koosch informed her of his two policies, a large one for Véronique, a smaller one for me.

Later on, Simone called my mother-in-law to discuss what Mr. Koosch had told her. She said that if they didn't give Véronique up right then, she was going to involve the police. My parents-in-law didn't want that. They told Simone they would bring Véronique to the hospital. Lenore told me, "We were afraid that they would take Véronique to Canada and that would be it. We would never see her again." To this day, I feel that money was the only reason my family wanted custody of Véronique.

My parents-in-law came to the hospital with my daughter. Corky Kuhlman and his wife, Karen, drove my car to the hospital with Boomer in it. When they walked into my room, Véronique and her aunt, Karen, were holding each other's hands. Simone grabbed Véronique, put her in the bathroom and wouldn't let her out. She screamed at Karen, "I'm going to get you." Simone didn't want the Kuhlman family near Véronique anymore.

At this point, the Kuhlmans all became upset. They kept saying, "We want to see Véronique. Let her out. What are you doing?" Simone was yelling at them, but finally a doctor went to get a security guard.

When the security guard entered, he asked what was going on. Corky answered, "We want to see Véronique before we go." Simone held Karen by her shirt and kept telling her, "You steal from Odette, I'm going to fix you." The security guard managed to separate Simone and Karen, and finally the Kuhlman family left.

When my brain worked better, I also learned from the Kuhlmans that they came to see me one day later at the hospital. They had previously visited every day. When they arrived at the Intensive Care ward, a registered nurse told my mother-in-law that the Kuhlman family wasn't allowed to see me anymore. Simone had instructed my doctor to limit visitors to her and my mother.

In addition, the nurse explained to my mother-in-law that Simone had asked Doctor Cucumb to transfer me to a French hospital in Québec, Canada. Dr. Cucumb told Simone that when I awoke from the coma, depending on my medical condition and how I felt, he would let her know if he could release me.

From friends in Los Angeles, I learned more about my family's so-called help. Friends invited my mother and Simone for dinners during their stay in Los Angeles. They told me, "We certainly had a taste of your sister, Simone."

One day, Marilyn had invited Mom and Simone for dinner. Marilyn's son, Alan, telephoned his mother. He already knew about the accident. Alan and I had been good friends; he now lives in another state. Alan told his mom that he had spoken with one of his friends who is an attorney. This attorney told Alan that my family should file a lawsuit against the State of California because it had been revealed that in the period of one week, six other people fell in the same canyon that winter.

He had the name of a lawyer in Los Angeles to give to my sister. Marilyn let Simone talk with Alan. After she took the information about this personal injury attorney, Alan told Simone that the lawsuit could be worth millions of dollars. The next morning Simone called the lawyer in Los Angeles and started action right away against the State of California.

My mother and sister wanted me to be hospitalized in Québec, Canada. Simone talked with my doctor one more time about it. Dr. Cucumb informed her that I was starting to awake from the coma and could be released on the condition that I travel with a registered nurse. Ambulances would have to take me to the airport in Los Angeles, and from the Québec airport to the hospital immediately. He would give the registered nurse my file, plus instructions on how to administer my medication.

My mother and sister then called my brother, René, and asked him to come to Los Angeles to help move me. René came right away. On January 14th, 1983, I was released from Kyung Ok Hospital for a seven-hour flight to Québec City. I don't remember anything about it. I was functioning like a robot again, completely unaware of the intrigue of my situation.

When I finally awoke in the French hospital in Lévis, I spoke with my sister, Simone, on the telephone. "I haven't seen you for a long time," I said. "When are you coming to see me?"

"I was with you in Los Angeles at the hospital all the time," she answered.

"I never saw you."

When I was released from the French hospital, and had returned to Los Angeles with Dustin, we visited my attorney, Mr. Koosch, who had met with my mother and Simone. I learned from him that Simone had been in Los Angeles at the medical center when I was comatose. I was also informed that one day when I seemed to be emerging from the coma, she immediately had me sign a Power of Attorney. Maybe she made me wake up long enough to sign. Maybe she steered my hand, who knows? Even though I was unable to read and write and have no recollection of anything, she had me sign the form. Many people repeated that statement to me. It was difficult for me to believe that anyone, particularly someone from my own family, would use this situation to try to take advantage of me. When I was informed of this, I could hardly believe what I was hearing. Many months later, when I visited my primary physician, Dr. Cucumb, he certified the misconduct of my family members.

In addition, I learned that before her departure from California, when Simone went to visit Mr. Koosch, she wanted the money that John left me following his death. Mr. Koosch told her, "I won't give you anything. When Mrs. Kuhlman comes back to California, she'll receive what belongs to her."

Later that year, Mr. Koosch told me how many problems he had with Simone and mother. They demanded John's life insurance money, his salary and everything else they could get their hands on."My employees had to help me throw them out of my office," he said.

When Simone realized that she could not get any more of my personal property in California, she returned to Ottawa, Canada, where my friend, Dustin, had been administrator of my affairs for six years. He held a Power of Attorney signed by me nine months prior to my accident. When Simone arrived at Loyola Trust to cash my Certificates of Deposit, my administrator, Dustin, said, "I was already there waiting for her. She could not get any money out of your Loyola Trust account, but she got twenty one thousand dollars from your Warrant Trust C.D. accounts."

Dustin also said, "When Simone was in Los Angeles with your mother, they would call me regularly to say they needed more money for hotel and other expenses. I answered their demands, Odette Marie. Simone and your mother asked for nine thousand five hundred dollars for their expenses in California. According to Simone, it was urgent that I send her money. Some of this amount was sent to them because of their insistence that it was an emergency and their demands. For the balance, Simone served herself when she came to Ottawa. She went to your savings and took what she wanted. I couldn't stop her because she had the Power of Attorney that she made you sign. Even though this paper was illegal, in Ottawa they didn't know about it." His story shocked me. I could hardly believe that my sister and mother were in California just to enjoy money that they were stealing from my daughter and I while I was in the coma.

Later on, in April 1983, I struggled to write Simone a letter. It was difficult because I didn't remember how to write, think clearly, or spell. I wrote words by the way they sounded. I asked her for all the money back, plus all receipts for the expenses from the nine thousand five hundred dollars for the fourteen days they spent in Los Angeles. She never answered my letter.

Through my attorney, Mr. Koosch, both my family and in-laws knew how much money my daughter and I would get from John's life insurance. I fear that my family was not in Los Angeles to help me because I was dying or because they loved me, but only because they wanted to know what they could get out of this accident. They were helping themselves. But, Véronique and I didn't know that yet.

At the hospital in Lévis I was unconscious (in a coma) until I finally woke up completely in the French mental facility and saw my darling daughter. If it wasn't for the fact that Véronique needed her mother, I would have stayed in the coma and not learned about my family's idea of helping.

I don't remember if Mom would come to see me every day. But, my brother, René, or my sister, Cécile, would be there in the afternoon, or at the evening visiting time. One day, René told me, "Cécile went to Los Angeles with Mom and Simone, but because of too many arguments with Simone, she came back to Canada after two days. I went to Los Angeles to help bring you to this hospital."

At this time René and Cécile told me several times during their visit that Simone had made me sign a Power of Attorney, and returned to Ottawa to steal my invested money. At first, I didn't understand what they were talking about, or why they were telling me that. I knew only that I was alive. That was the important thing. I finally told Cécile and René, "What assets I have are all for Véronique. Nobody can touch anything."

"But Simone made you sign a Power of Attorney in the Kyung Ok Hospital and she used it to get money from your savings in Ottawa." They would then say, "Do you understand?"

A couple of months later, in March of 1983, I understood. This illegal Power of Attorney was signed January 8th, supposedly by me, and, with Dustin's help, I was able to revoke it at the end of March.

When you enter into a coma following brain damage, you escape to a peaceful world. No one should take advantage of this quiet period of time that your brain chooses to relax and escape from pain. Nobody, especially your family, should make you sign papers when you don't even exist mentally. My brain had shut down to protect itself. All the time I was in the French hospital, I was in a heightened state of confusion with a severely decreased ability to process information. I was detached from the present and responded primarily to my own internal worries. I was never fully aware of present events.

Another of my sisters, Ruth, often came to see me in the hospital. She was always warm and nice to me. My older brother, Steven, didn't come often, but it was okay, because I didn't remember him enough to miss him.

During my three-week hospitalization, Dr. Compre, the psychiatrist, came to see me one morning and, after checking on my progress, said, "Your family is calling all the time, especially

Cécile, who wants you to be released from here. She would like you to stay at her home with your daughter."

Finally, when I was released from the French hospital in February, Cécile brought me to her home where I was reunited with my daughter, Véronique. Even though my ability to think, walk, and cook were limited, my psychiatrist, Dr. Compre, said I was capable of living with my daughter while I received the medical treatment necessary for my recuperation. He told my family that it was important that Véronique and I be together. My love for Véronique became the reason I wanted to return to health. For Cécile and René this didn't matter. What was important for my daughter and I didn't matter. What they could get financially from us was their main focus.

At the time, Véronique and I were innocent, not realizing my own family wanted the life insurance my young daughter would receive. Later, I learned that Cécile and René were in financial trouble. By doing what they could to keep me in a mental institution, Cécile could use our money to save her business and secure our brother from financial failure.

After a short time, my brother, René, came to Cécile's home and told me that I should go with him to his home. He didn't say anything about Véronique going, instead he acted like Cécile was going to keep her.

"René, I have to prepare Véronique to come with us." Cécile looked at me and said, "Véronique is going to stay here."

"I'm not going with René if my daughter does not come with me," I said.

Now an argument started about who would keep my daughter. Cécile could not understand the need that Véronique and I had to be together. The only thing she could do was argue. I decided to go see Dr. Compre and see Véronique's psychiatrist, Dr. Boussel. Cécile and René insisted that they come with me, and they did. When the doctor came to get us in the waiting room at the hospital, Cécile wanted to come in with me.

"I want to see you alone," I said. "If I can't, forget it. I made the appointment; they didn't."

Dr. Boussel realized that I was serious. "No problem, Mrs. Kuhlman. Come into my office."

Dr. Compre joined us and I explained to them that I wanted to live my life with my daughter like I had done since the day she was born. This was very important to me.

"Madame Kuhlman, that is your decision," they said.
I told them how Cécile did not want me to take care of my child. Both doctors said, "Your sister, Cécile, can't do anything about it. The decision is in your hands. She can't do anything against that."

Dr. Boussel went to get Cécile and René. When they came into the doctor's office, Dr. Compre told them what I wanted. Cécile said, "But, Odette Marie is unable to take care of her daughter. What could we do to keep Véronique?"

"You could organize a family meeting," Dr. Compre said. "If Madame Kuhlman's family votes for you, you could keep her child. It would depend on what the family decides."

René looked at the doctors and said, "No. We had a family meeting once to vote about my father, and I would never do that again."

By refusing to do what Cécile wanted, René saved my physical, intellectual and emotional life. I could not have survived without Véronique. She was the reason I had willed myself back from the coma, my reason to live. I could never thank him enough for his gesture of sympathy.

When we left the doctor's office and went back to Cécile's residence, I talked with my daughter in our bedroom, in private. "We are going to move to René's house."

Cécile came to the door and said, "It's a big mistake, Odette Marie, because you're mentally sick."

Suddenly I realized why they had put me in the mental ward of the hospital. They wanted to adopt Véronique because of her insurance inheritance. They could prove that I would be mentally unable to take care of her.

I walked over to Cécile. "Leave my daughter with me." I asked her, "What would you do if someone tried to do this to your son?"

In the living room, she argued more and jumped at me, took me by my neck and pushed me against the rocks of the fireplace. She held me in that position for a long time. My mother was in the kitchen, but came into the living room when she heard us argue.

"What happened? What are you doing?" Cécile finally let me go and I fell on the sofa. Cécile stepped to the side of the living room, still angry.

I got up to get my daughter in the bedroom and, when I reached the upper stairway, my sister pushed me down the stairs. Falling, I tried to hold the stairwell to protect myself. Just then René arrived, and saw me lying at the foot of the stairs. He came over and picked me up. He walked me to his automobile outside, near the front door of the house, and returned to get Véronique while I waited outside. I was very upset . . . It reminded me of how cruel she used to be when we were children. I became very afraid of her. In my heart I felt she would stop at nothing to get what she wanted. We arrived at René's home and met his family. Even though I knew his son, Marc, since he was born, I could not remember him because of my injury. I had never before met Paulette, his companion, but it didn't seem to matter. They were very kind to Véronique and me, always there to help us. René took good care of us.

During the time we were living at René's home, Dustin called me regularly from Ottawa to find out how I was. He wanted me to know that I had some business papers at his home that I would have to take care of before I returned to Los Angeles. He also invited us to spend some time at his residence. So, I told René that Véronique and I were going to stay at Dustin's in Ottawa for a few days and that we would be back. Dustin would pick us up on Friday. René agreed.

Friday arrived and so did Dustin. We were prepared to go. Just before we left, René turned to me and said, "Odette Marie, I have your jewels. They are at the bank, but it is closed now."

"When I come back, be sure to give them to me," I said.

"All right, don't worry about it. Monday, I'll go to the bank to get everything for you."

When we arrived at Dustin's home, his wife Sylvie, who is also my sister, and his children welcomed us very warmly. She immediately prepared a bedroom downstairs for us. During the three weeks we were there, I was still afraid of my family. I couldn't believe what they were trying to do to my daughter and me. But at Dustin's, I felt safe. I knew that no one could touch us there.

While I was there one morning at breakfast, the telephone rang. It was my sister, Cécile, asking me to pay for the airplane tickets that Mom, René, Simone and she bought to go to Los Angeles when I was comatose following the mountain accident. She also asked me to pay her two thousand dollars that Simone had borrowed from her.

"I'll pay you for the tickets, but Mom and Simone each had a free pass with the airline because Simone works there. And, I'm not going to pay the loan that you made to Simone. I'm not responsible if your sister borrowed money from you or anyone else."

"All right, Odette Marie. I'll manage another way to get my money back," she snapped.

One hour later, my brother René called and said, "If you don't pay Cécile the 2,000 dollars that Simone borrowed, I'll take all of your jewelry, go into the street, and sell it." He was talking about twenty five thousand dollars worth of jewelry. At the time, I didn't even know how he got his hands on it.

"You can't do that, René. Those jewels are my property. John gave them to me." He started arguing and said, "You don't know me. I'll do it."

I hung up the phone, amazed, angry and hurt. Simone's greed had finally gotten to him. René called back the next day and asked when Cécile was going to get paid. I was emotionally unable to talk to him, so Sylvie, Dustin's wife, took the phone. She told him that Simone's loan wasn't supposed to be paid by me, that they couldn't ask for money that I never touched, never saw. René just argued and created more problems for poor Sylvie. Finally, she did what I would have done, she hung up the telephone.

"Sylvie, I don't want René to sell my jewelry. John gave it to me when he was alive. It should go to Véronique and to nobody else." This was very important to me.

Through her patient listening, Sylvie helped me very much. She told me she understood everything, but she didn't know what she could do.

One day later, Cécile and René called again to find out if I was going to pay Simone's loan, or, if they would have to sell my jewelry on the street.

"Tell them that I'll pay, Sylvie, because I want my jewelry

back."

Then Cécile asked to talk to me. "Here's how we will handle this, Odette Marie. Come to my home Saturday night with the money to pay Simone's loan, and we will give you your jewelry."

"I already sent you a check to pay all the airplane tickets. I'll bring the money for Simone's loan. I have to see if Dustin can drive me. It is three hundred miles away."

"If you want your jewelry, you better be here Saturday," Cécile responded.

When Dustin arrived home from work, I told him what had happened.

"I'll drive you there, Odette Marie," Dustin said.

On Saturday, we drove to Cécile's home in Lévis. On the way, Dustin remarked, "It's not worth living when members of your family act this way."

I agreed. I was terribly hurt. "Do you know where and how they got my jewelry?"

"When you were comatose in the Los Angeles hospital, they went to your home and helped themselves," Dustin said.

We arrived at Cécile's residence. My brother, René, was there too. Her boyfriend, Arman, was also present.

"Come into my office," Cécile said.

René, Dustin and I went into her office where she told us to sit down and closed the door.

"I want you to pay me for everything," she said.

I told her that I had already paid her for all (4) airline tickets. She looked at the check I had sent and said, "This check isn't good. It is signed by your friend, Dustin. Make me another check, sign it and you will receive everything after that."

I looked at Dustin.

"Try to make them another check," he said.
I started to write even though it was very difficult. I was still unable to write, shaking and very nervous. I could not remember how to write anymore.

Finally, Cécile stood up. "I'll print the check and you sign."

When I did, René handed me one ring. "Take this," he said.

"No, I want everything."

"We can't give you all your jewelry," he said.

"We're going to keep your jewelry until your check clears at the bank," Cécile yelled.

I cried, "I want my wedding ring!" René took back the one ring that he had previously given me, and handed me my wedding ring.

While Dustin and I were getting prepared to exit her office, Cécile said, "Why don't you file a lawsuit action against Simone. We'll help you."

"I'll go to court if your attorney needs me," said René.
Heartbroken, I left with Dustin. My sister, Cécile, and René kept my jewelry. That was in March 1983, only two months after I awoke from the coma.

"Your Mother invited us to go sleep at her home," Dustin said as we drove away.

"I wonder why?" I asked. "Does she know what her two other children did to me?"

"I'm not sure what she knows exactly," Dustin said. "But she's aware that we would be at Cécile's tonight. She doesn't want us to drive all the way back to Ottawa and told me we could sleep at her house."

So we went to mother's, and when she saw me, she said, "Is everything fine, Odette Marie?"

I told her what Cécile and René did to me.

"Did you get your jewelry?"

They want the check to clear at Warrant Trust before they give Odette Marie her jewelry," Dustin said.

"They'll send it to you. I'm sure," my mother said.

"Yes, mother, but they sold me jewelry that my husband gave me before he died." I cried.

"It's correct. You're going to get everything back," my mother said.

"Mother, they stole my personal property!"

"They aren't stealing anything, they only took their salary for the time they were in Los Angeles."

My mother could never understand the logic of this situation. Simone had influenced her. They were a team. I had to pay their debts. My mother would protect Simone always, as she had done all her life.

Mother told us that she had prepared our beds and showed us to our rooms. Dustin went to the blue bedroom and I went to the beige one. I couldn't undress, I was so upset and afraid. Everything that my family was trying to do to my daughter and me since my fall seemed inhuman. My brain was reeling.

I cried to Dustin, "I'm afraid to sleep, I may die!"

"Try to sleep," he tried to calm me. "I feel that way sometimes, but it goes away."

"I'll be on the same floor as you. If you need something, just call me."

The next morning we left to go back to his home in Ottawa. During the trip, Dustin told me, "Odette Marie, if I were you, I would consult an attorney regarding the acts of René, Cécile and Simone. I know a good lawyer where I live. If you want, I'll make an appointment for you."

"I would like my family to reimburse me for all the money they stole from my daughter and me. This is terrible, what they did."

"Tomorrow I'll called this attorney, Mr. Anderson, and we'll see him this week," Dustin said.

While we were back in Ottawa, Dustin's wife, Sylvie, came to me and said, "If you want, today I"ll let you drive my car. Do you remember how to drive?"

I wasn't sure, but I was willing to try it. She explained to me how to start the car as she started her automobile. Then she showed me the gas pedal and the brake. I had to be shown these things again.

"Why do we signal when we turn left or right, and make a stop by a sign?" I asked.

She showed me every important movement in order to drive safely. After the first demonstration, she parked her car on the side of the street, turned off the engine and we changed places.

"Here we go," she said. "Now you try it."

It was my turn to give her a ride. I have to say that she was quite brave. I was more scared then she, or if she was afraid, she didn't show it. She told me to signal before I changed lanes and kept me on a straight road for a while. Then she decided to give me more action. "Signal to the left," she said. "At the next street, you're going to turn left."

I did just what she wanted me to do.

"Go back straight on the road. Stay to the right and I'll tell you when to turn," I drove with Sylvie's help for an hour. Then she told me, "You're on your own." I had to decide where I wanted to go, where I wanted to turn. I thought that I was doing well, but my co-driver at one point told me, "You're driving much too fast. You're going to kill us. Keep to your right and don't go faster than 20 miles an hour." I was so excited, my right foot was heavy on the gas pedal, and my left foot was always prepared to push the brake. But as far as I was concerned, I had done it. I had relearned how to drive. That was enough.

"You did well, but let's go home," Sylvie said. "We can do it again another time." I drove her home, but that was it. I didn't drive anymore while I was in Canada. On March 7th, 1983, Dustin and I went to see Mr. Anderson, the attorney. Dustin explained what had happened to my daughter, my husband and I during the mountain accident in California. The lawyer asked who had come to see me in Los Angeles. Dustin answered, "Odette Marie's mother, two of her sisters and one of her brothers went to Los Angeles to see her. They went to get Odette Marie's signature on the Power of Attorney forms while she was comatose."

"It looks like you have a civil and criminal action lawsuit here," Mr. Anderson said. "It'll be expensive to sue them, because they acted in another country. You would need a lawyer in Los Angeles and us here to represent you. Would you sue all of them?"

"I wouldn't sue mother," I said. "Only because she is my Mom. When I was young, my father always told me, 'You don't have to love your mother, but you must respect her. She is your mother.' So, I would consider taking action only against René, Cécile and Simone."

Dustin asked Mr. Anderson, "Could you write to Simone and ask for a breakdown of the 9,500 dollars expenses they say occurred during the fourteen days she was in Los Angeles?"

The attorney said he would write her before taking the lawsuit action. Before leaving his office, I told Mr. Anderson, "Dustin and I are going to talk about the civil and criminal action against my family and we'll call you back to inform you what we decide to do." On March 8th, 1983, he sent a letter to Simone requesting a breakdown of the expenses.

The next day, there was a call from an attorney from California. "Mrs. Kuhlman, I'm Mr. Koocsh, your attorney from Los Angeles. I want to know how you are and I also want to tell you that your divorce would have been final this week."

"Do I know you?" I asked.

"Yes, I'm the attorney who was taking care of your divorce," he said.

"Everybody tells me that John is dead, but I don't know if it's true," I said.

"Yes, John is dead," he said. "He won't be a problem to you and your daughter any more. When are you coming back to California?"

"I don't know."

"Write down my telephone number and my name. When you arrive in Los Angeles, give me a call. I need to speak to you regarding your husband."

When Dustin arrived from work, I told him about the Los Angeles attorney. "Is it true I was asking for a divorce?" I asked.

"Yes, Odette Marie, you were definitively asking for it," my friend responded.

"I love John. Why was I asking for a divorce?"

"John told you if you refused to return Véronique to Korea, he would leave you," Dustin said. "He couldn't live with both of you. It had been three years since John and you were living apart. After he asked you to choose, you went in psychotherapy for a while and then decided to ask for a divorce. You chose your daughter. Véronique was just three years old then. But don't worry, I'll go with you to see this attorney," Dustin added.

The same day that Mr. Koocsh had called, my mother-in-law also called. "Odette Marie, sweetheart," she said, "I'm sorry to disturb you, but it's important that I talk with you. John is in a freezer at Schetman Mortuary and they just called here to tell us that they can't keep his body any longer. He's been dead over two and a half months and you have to do something with the body otherwise they'll cremate him."

"Would you call the mortuary to tell them to keep John a few more days, and I'll be there to identify him? Lenore, tell them that I must see John. They must keep him. I promise, I'll be there."

She agreed.

I discussed the call with Dustin and asked him, "Would you come with me to Los Angeles? I have to take care of John, and I'm afraid to see him dead. I have to go there this week otherwise they will throw John away."

"Let me make airline reservations for tomorrow, if possible. You can call Lenore back and tell her that we'll be in Los Angeles for sure this week. Tell her to inform the mortician. They'll keep John for you."

When I called Lenore back, she told me, "Honey, you should call the mortuary where Johnny is to tell them that you're coming to identify him. As his wife, they need you to call."

She gave me the phone number and I called right away, explaining who I was. I told the man, "I can't believe that my husband is dead and I need to see his body. Would you please keep John for me and my daughter?"

The mortician agreed to keep John's body frozen until I could see him. He gave me the address and told me he would wait two more days.

After the conversation, I asked Dustin not to say anything to my mother or anyone in the family about Véronique and my departure to California. I was afraid that Cécile would kidnap Véronique for her money. Dustin assured me that no one except his family would know. We left Ottawa in the middle of March, 1983.

<h1 style="text-align:center">CHAPTER 6 - RELEASE</h1>

I felt that the scenario of my first life was finished. The only good feeling I had was my love for my daughter, Véronique. I also cared very deeply for my confrère, Dustin. Without these two people, I had absolutely nothing to live for. We flew seven hours before arriving at Los Angeles International Airport where Dustin rented a car.

"Can you drive us to your home?" he asked.

"Don't worry. You take care of Véronique and the luggage and I'll drive us home. I think I remember how."

I was scared, but I couldn't let it show. My insides were telling me that I had to survive, I had to do it. I did remember that I had to take the 405 Freeway North, and another freeway following that. I couldn't remember which one it was. I drove until we arrived at the top of a canyon overlooking a panoramic display of beautiful lights. Then, I saw a green sign for the 101 Freeway West and I entered that road. When we arrived in Thousand Oaks, Véronique remembered where to exit, and which road to take to go home. The difference between driving in Ottawa and driving in Los Angeles is the size of the road and the number of cars on it. In Ottawa I relearned how to drive on a Sunday morning when everybody was at church. There was no traffic, and only two lanes to deal with. That was easy and fun. In Los Angeles, the puzzle was bigger. There were five lanes of freeway instead of one, and a lot of traffic.

The challenge was bigger, but with the help of Dustin and Véronique, I did it. By the time we arrived at my residence in Thousand Oaks, we were all exhausted. When we entered the front room of the house, it felt strange to me; a new decor. My memory had been entirely erased. I could not remember my own home. Véronique acted as my new memory.

The next morning, I drove Véronique to Madrona School and spoke with the director. She went back to the classroom where she was before the accident. During that time, Dustin called the mortician to find out what time we could see John. He made an appointment for the following morning. He then called the attorney, Mr. Koosch, to meet him the same day that we would be at the mortuary in Torrance. When Véronique came back from school, I spoke with her. "Mama and Dustin are going to go see Daddy at the mortuary tomorrow. Would you like to come with us?"

"Mama, I can't go see Daddy, but I'll make him a picture, if you want to give it to Daddy."

"Fine, Mama will give Daddy your picture and I'm going to give him a letter that I wrote."

The following morning, Dustin and I dropped Véronique at school, and then went to Torrance to the mortuary. As we got out of the car I said, "I'm so afraid, I'm afraid of seeing John dead."

"Come on, I'm scared too. I've never done this before," Dustin said.

We went in and the mortician greeted us politely. "Please wait in my office, I'll prepare your husband so you can see him."

He served us some coffee. I held Dustin tightly. We were both very nervous and afraid. A few minutes later, the mortician returned. "You can see Mr. Kuhlman now. Just follow me."

I squeezed Dustin's hand. When we entered the room, Dustin gasped. "This isn't John. He never had a beard."

"Can I walk closer to my husband?" I asked.

"Yes."

I approached the body and opened my purse to take out Véronique's picture and the letter I had written for John. I slowly lifted the white sheet and put them on John's chest.

"What are you doing? Don't touch him," the mortician said.

"I'm giving my husband two gifts. A picture that my daughter wanted her Dad to have, and a letter that I wrote him."

"Fine, you can put this on him, but don't touch his body." The mortician explained that the body could easily crumble after being kept for so long.

I stayed beside John, staring at his body and feeling how much love I had for that man. I was unable to cry. Internally, I was lost. His hair was long and curly, touching his shoulders. His beard had grown long, down to his chest. I stood there paralyzed beside John, not knowing what I felt. I just admired his face. He was so beautiful. The mortician approached me, held my shoulder and said, "Mrs. Kuhlman, I would like to give you some coffee. Would you come in my office? We will talk together."

I went with him and Dustin followed. When we entered his office, the mortician asked me what I wanted to do with John's body.

"We would like him to be cremated," Dustin said. "Could you take care of that? John is to be buried in Québec, Canada. When I return to Canada, I'll take John's ashes with me. Is it permissible to carry the ashes in a suitcase?"

"Yes," The mortician answered. He gave the dimension of the box that John's ashes would be put in.

"Won't I need some papers telling what I have in the box. When I pass immigration in Toronto, I don't want to have any problems."

"Mr. Kuhlman won't be cremated here at this facility, but I'll take care of everything for you. I'll give you a permit for disposition of human remains. All Mr. Kuhlman's information will be on it. You won't have any difficulty."

Dustin paid the mortician for the time that John's body was kept in the freezer, plus the cost for the cremation.

"You can come back in three days and everything will be ready," the mortician told us.

"Sir, before I leave, I would like to ask you a question," Dustin said. "John didn't have a beard and long hair. Now all his hair is so long, what happened?"

"Even when you are dead your hair and beard still have the capacity to grow. This is why Mr. Kuhlman has so much hair.

It's been two and a half months since he died and we haven't used any chemicals on the body."

As we left the mortuary, Dustin and I hugged each other. Our faces were pale, white, like snow. "I don't want to come back with you to get John," I said. "I dislike this place."

"Don't worry, Odette Marie, I'll come alone. John's remains will be in a box," he said.
"Now we're going to visit Mr. Koosch, the lawyer. It's about 5 miles from here. I talked with him yesterday and he's expecting us."

When we arrived at Mr. Koosch's office, he greeted us politely. Dustin introduced himself, but Mr. Koosch recognized me.

"Don't you remember me, Mrs. Kuhlman?"

"No, I really don't know who you are."

"Where is Véronique and how is she?"

"Véronique is at school and she is fine."

We sat down in his office and Mr. Koosch told us the details.

"John had two life insurance policies and this week you'll receive money from them. Also, Mrs. Kuhlman, you'll need to come with me to court in downtown Los Angeles regarding the guardianship of your daughter." He gave Dustin instructions on how to get to Astrolune Co., where John worked before his death. He explained that even though John was dead, Véronique and I were still insured under his company's health insurance plan. We would be insured for one year by the company without having to pay for it.

We needed to go to Astrolune Co. to collect John's last payroll check and to John's bank to close his account. Mr. Koosch gave Dustin a letter so that we could cash his payroll check and close the bank account without John's signature. He also advised me that it would be a good idea to pay John's attorney for the time she spent on the divorce preparation. I agreed and told my attorney to inform John's lawyer that I would cover her expenses.

Functioning throughout that day was very difficult. I felt like a robot instead of a real human, just going through the motions necessary. Without Dustin, I would never have been able to do all that was required to work through the close of my former life. He was a godsend to me. As I look back, I realize that he helped me see that I must survive, put away the painful past, and move on to wellness.

During this time, Dustin had to repeat to me what people were saying and why. I couldn't remember anything. At the end of that particular day, I was still confused, left in the dark. This is why Dustin decided to write down all the information for me. He told Véronique and me, "When I'm back in Canada, if you want to know what we did together since John died, Véronique can just look at the paper and read it to you. Or, you can ask a friend to read it to you. This is the best I can do for you now."

The day after we had taken care of all the mortuary arrangements was March 25th, 1983. Véronique cried again this morning. She asked me if Daddy was beautiful yesterday when we viewed his body, and then she cried again. She was very nervous and upset, and refused to talk about the accident.

Before he left, Dustin and I drove to John's apartment in Northridge. When we arrived at the manager's office, I introduced myself, told her that John was dead, and asked for a key to his apartment to pack his things. I showed her my driver's license and my marriage certificate. But, it wasn't enough.

"I'll go in with you," she said, "but I'm not going to give you Mr. Kuhlman's apartment key. And you can't move any of his personal property out of his apartment. If you show me a death certificate and a letter from a lawyer that authorizes you to move Mr. Kuhlman's furniture, fine. But we also need to be paid for the last three months."

"We'll come back on Friday," Dustin said. "We'll have the money to cover the rent for the last three months and we'll bring the letter you need from Mrs. Kuhlman's lawyer."

"Fine, you can come with me now to see Mr. Kuhlman's apartment."

When we entered John's apartment, I went to his bedroom where I found the wedding ring that I had given him at our wedding on July 24th, 1971. The manager allowed me to keep the ring and I was grateful.

Back at home, Dustin called Mr. Koosch for a letter explaining John's death to the landlord. He also called one of John's friends, and asked him if he could help us move John's engineering equipment on Saturday. Dennis Moore and his wife, Anita, agreed to help us.

Friday morning, Dustin and I went to pick up John's remains. I stayed in the car while Dustin handled that. We picked up the letter at Mr. Koosch's office and returned to Northridge to pay John's landlord and start packing. It took two days to complete, with the help of John's friends. I asked the apartment manager if she could donate the remainder of John's furniture to poor people who might need it. She said she would. A moving company picked up John's computer, his office furniture and all his clothes. This felt like one last phase of my husband's life that Dustin and I were closing.

When we returned home, Dustin asked me, "Where do you want me to put John's ashes?"

"Not in my bedroom. Put him where I can't see him, I'm too afraid. Véronique said, "Mother, I'm also afraid. I don't want to see Daddy dead in our home."

"Okay, I'll put him under the bed where I sleep. So, don't be afraid, I'll watch him," Dustin said.

While in California, Dustin slept in Véronique's bedroom and my daughter and I shared the master bedroom. Even though we knew that Dustin was sleeping with John's ashes in the other room, we were both still uneasy.

When the day came for Dustin to go back to Canada, he said, "If you had ever told me that one day I would carry John in my suitcase, I would never have believed you. This is just unbelievable."

"What are you going to do with John?"

"I'll keep him at home in my office until you come to bury him. But, don't take too long."

Dustin called us every week after his departure from Los Angeles. In this beginning of my second life, I just didn't know what to do with my deceased husband. I didn't want John to be alone. When my father was alive, he and John were good friends. I believe this is why I asked if I could bury John in the Bourget family plot. Four months later, in July of 1983, I flew alone to Québec, Canada, to bury my husband. My mother had authorized me to do it.

After the funeral, Mother invited everyone to her home. When we arrived there, Dustin said to me, "Come with me to your mother's bedroom. I've received your jewelry back from Cécile and René. Check to see that everything is there."

Nothing was missing, but I could not forget that it cost me 5,000 dollars to buy back what John, my husband, had given me when he was alive. I don't remember who was at the funeral. But, I know for sure that my sisters, Cécile and Simone, and my brother, René, were not present. I never saw them again after they stole from my daughter and me.

The day of the funeral, I told Dustin to call the attorney, Mr. Anderson, in Ottawa, and tell him that I would not sue my sisters and brother. God would take care of them. It would only be a question of time.

During the two weeks that Dustin was in Los Angeles helping me, many of my girlfriends invited us for dinner. They could not believe what had happened to John, Véronique and me. They said I was lucky to be alive, my injuries were so severe. It was more than a tragedy to us; it was a nightmare. Some of my Californian friends with their husbands and children helped Dustin, Véronique, and me greatly at this time. Others invited us for dinner only because Simone told them my deceased husband had left us money from his life insurance policies. Still others thought that I was going to become a millionaire through the lawsuit that Simone and my mother had filed against the State of California for negligence. At a time like this, you really learn who your true family and friends are.

CHAPTER 7 - BEGINNING MY SECOND LIFE

Having a second chance at life, I believe, can be wonderful. But starting it like I did, you wonder if it is humanly possible. I received more love and understanding from friends and strangers than from my family. Every night I prayed and asked God, "Why did you allow that accident to happen? Why was I cursed with such terrible family members?" I spoke to my Dad in my thoughts, asking him what happened to the family that he had loved and cared for so much? Why were they acting like this? Why did they need to hurt me?

Giving and sharing are the most beautiful things in life. You can do it for anyone. You don't have to be related to the person. You can share a smile with a stranger; just simply be nice to people. We should take time to understand and help other people. I have been so close to death that I have learned how important life is. Nothing else matters. Not money or material things. Even if you're poor, it isn't important. What is important is your health. It doesn't cost anything to show love, affection and to communicate.

From the time I awoke from the coma, my body and my soul craved so much love and attention . . . it was incredible. I felt that I didn't have enough friends, and I feared that the ones that I had would die too. For me, being alone in a large country like the United States of America, in the state of California, was very difficult. Without my daughter and my friends, I don't know what I would have done.

I had come so close to dying. And, I had come back to life to face a terrible ordeal. I would watch television, go shopping, just look at people, and think, "Why are they doing this? Why are they buying that? They don't realize, but they could be dead in a second. It could happen so fast."

I remember my daughter asking me to watch a Jerry Lewis movie on television. It was difficult to relate to a funny movie. I wondered how the actors could have so much fun. Didn't they realize they could be dead in a second? I was filled with fear, so afraid to die . . . it was unbelievable. I couldn't tell my daughter what I felt, because she would have been scared too. I didn't want to burden her that way.

By 1984, I was still afraid. I prayed to God to keep me alive; I wanted to finish raising my daughter and become a grandmother. I desperately wanted to forget about dying.

Sometimes, Véronique would say, "Mom, I'm alive because you adopted me from Korea. And you're alive because I saved your life. I called loudly to get some help. Mother, I saved you." I told her how lucky I was to have her, and that I loved her the most in the world. I wanted God to keep me alive with her.

Becoming a widow was another painful experience. For a while, I couldn't believe that John was dead. My memory was severely impaired, with confusion of past and present, and impatient reactions to ongoing activity. I lacked short term recall and I often flashed back to past events. My past memories showed more depth and detail than any recent memory.

Not many people understood how confused I was. My greatest concern was the physical injury that created my loss of memory, and retrieving healthy functioning brain cells. I could remember scenes from my childhood and my teenage days, but I could only remember a part of my adult life. Every day that God would give me, I would relive my past, but it wasn't easy. It was just too much for the left side of my brain to handle.

The left side of my brain wanted to be normal with all its physical, intellectual, and mental capacities, but the right side of my brain could not function anymore at the same level as before. I was stuck in the middle. The two sides of my brain couldn't work in unison, like they had for my first 37 years. I felt like my brain was full of water, as though it were floating in the ocean. I could feel the waves, and was very scared by it.

Small things were upsetting to me. I struggled to remember and understand. At first my brain didn't know why I had hair on my legs, what it was to be menstruating. When I first saw my menstrual blood, I had to ask what was wrong with me.

At the hospital in Lévis, my sister, Cécile, brought a razor and said to me, "Shave your legs, shave your underarms also." After she left the hospital, I went to the bathroom and looked in the mirror. I didn't see any hair under my arms. I kept asking myself, "Am I suppose to have hair there?" It was a mystery. I didn't remember that I'd had electrolysis done under my arms. That I would never have anymore hair there.

I remember the day Dustin and I went to John's apartment. Dustin had always prepared the freeway directions, and I would do the driving. Able or not, it was important to me. I had to survive. Someone had to do it, and Dustin decided that I could. I drove from Thousand Oaks to Northridge without any problems. He would tell me which freeway to take and which exit to use. I would always stay in the right lane of the freeway, prepared to pull over if I got too scared. Coming back home was a nightmare. Dustin had to drive John's car to my home in Thousand Oaks, and for the first time, I had to drive my car alone . . . no more co-driver. Dustin had written down the directions and said, "You just have to follow me." Easy to say, but impossible to do.

I followed him to the first freeway, the 118. But then I lost him. I was driving very slow, with other cars passing all around me. I had the paper with the directions, but I was unable to read since my accident. I was so lost, I drove to the end of the 118 freeway north and arrived in Moorpark. I asked at different gas stations where the 23 freeway to Thousand Oaks was located. The gentlemen would tell me how to get there, which road to take, but it was impossible for my brain to register the directions people gave me. I could hear, but nothing would register. I got back on the road and tried very hard to find the 23 freeway south, while looking at Dustin's directions again and again to see if I could find the way. Nothing would work.

At one point I stopped the car in the street to speak to someone that was walking. I asked him, "How do I get to Thousand Oaks? Which road do I take?" This man gave me directions to drive to Simi Valley first. From that city I could take the 23 freeway south. I drove to Simi Valley, but could not find the 23 freeway.

I stopped at private residences, knocked on the door, and asked whoever answered if he or she could help me. Over three hours had passed. I was really lost. Many people gave me directions and I thought I would be fine, but it didn't work. I was so mad at myself. I recalled that in the past I knew how to take all of these freeways without any help, but now I was stuck because of the accident. It wasn't fair that I was injured so severely. I didn't do anything wrong. I just wanted to save John. Why is God punishing me? I kept thinking, talking to myself, and trying to find the darn 23 freeway.

After a long period of time I stopped at another house. I told the couple what happened to me; how I was so lost and why I couldn't read the directions. "Would you please help me? I need to go home. I live in Thousand Oaks, and I don't remember how to go to my town." The couple was extremely kind. The lady told her husband to have me follow him to the 23 freeway. She explained to me that after a few miles, I'd see the 101 freeway west to Thousand Oaks. "Just take that freeway, watch for the Ventu Road exit, and you'll be home."

That was my last step. I followed her husband, took the 23 freeway south to the 101 and I finally arrived at my house. It had taken me a total of four hours to drive from Northridge to Thousand Oaks that day.

When I entered the house, Dustin was sitting on the sofa. He looked at me angrily and said, "Where have you been? What did you do? Damn it! Where did you go? I got lost on the freeway and had trouble getting back to your house!"

"I got lost too," I cried, "It's taken me four hours to find the right freeway."

I explained how difficult it was for me. "You're not the only one that got lost."

It didn't matter what I told him. He glared at me. "Odette Marie, you've lived here for 7 years and you can't drive on a freeway without being lost? Where is your sense of direction?"

"I've lost all my sense of direction," I said. "I can't even drive anymore. Just forget it, I'm sorry if I gave you problems," I told

Dustin.

We didn't speak to each other for two days. He was mad at me because I wasn't there to help him find the freeway. Friends often lose patience with brain injured persons. And I was mad at him because he could not see that since my injury, I had to relearn everything. After two days, we finally softened and apologized. Peace and friendship were still alive. As Dustin prepared to return to Canada, he asked my friends to help me after his departure.

My brain wanted so many answers that I was intellectually unable to give. It seemed that at 37 years old, I was reborn, obliged to relearn who I was. Why was I built this way? Why was I physically, intellectually and mentally limited this way on half of my brain. I had to discover who I was and try to relive the first life of Odette Marie Kuhlman.

This is what I call living with brain damage. Most of my family thought that I was mentally disturbed. They couldn't understand the physical damage, the injury to my brain. That was the reason that Cécile registered me in the mental ward of a French hospital. The family energy was concentrated on the mental aspect only.

When Simone and my mother filed a lawsuit against the State of California for $23 million according to them, I was just a vegetable. I wasn't supposed to survive. I suspect they thought, they had hit the jackpot.

CHAPTER 8 - VÉRONIQUE

My daughter expressed great psychological and physical pain after witnessing our accident in Angeles Crest Canyon on December 27th, 1982. During the time I was hospitalized at Kyung Ok Hospital in Los Angeles, and also the time I was hospitalized in l'Hôtel Dieu de Lévis in Québec, it was impossible for me to know or comprehend her anxiety and fear. Too many things were going on. Neither of us could concentrate on a cure for our physical and emotional pain.

After I was released from the hospital and left my family to return to California, Véronique, now seven years old, would tell me, "I'll defend you, mama. Nobody in your family will hurt you anymore."

During the first week she was back at school in California, we received a flyer in the mail from *Maurice Levesque Karate Studio.* It said, *Publicity to follow karate courses in Newbury Park.* I showed it to my daughter and asked what she thought about it. She said, "Mama, if you send me to these courses, I would be able to protect you better against your family." I made an appointment with Maurice Lévesque, director of the Art Karate Studio. Before going there, I specifically had a talk with Véronique concerning why she wanted to take Karate classes. I did not want her thinking she had to protect me.

"I would like you to follow this karate course for yourself. I don't want you to go there to protect mama. You should enjoy the course and do it only for you."

She said she understood, but said it would be for both of us.

She registered and classes started the same week. In the class, Véronique would use a big leather punching bag, striking it until she was exhausted. She learned many kicks from her teacher and I could see how much she needed the release. All her anger was directed toward Karate.

Every night after dinner, she would come to my bedroom or to the family room, depending on where I was, and bring a doll. She would hold it in her hand, raise her arm above her head and let the doll drop. Then, she would cry. I would ask her, "Véronique, sweetheart, tell mama what you are doing? Why are you crying?"

She would tell me, "This is what you did."

"What did I do, Véronique? Explain it to mama."

She wouldn't answer. She would take another doll, put it on the edge of the table and let it fall to the floor.

"Mama can't take what you're doing to your dolls. They will be hurt and broken. Would you stop doing that?"

She would stop for a few seconds and then, automatically, she would start all over again.

At one point, she took two dolls, put them on the back of a seat and let them fall to the floor, one after the other. I asked her to come to me. I wanted to hug her, but still couldn't walk very well. She was always there for me. She would come immediately. "Honey, you let your dolls fall and you never pick them up."

"Mom, I can't pick them up." I took her hand, walked over to the dolls and began to pick them up with her. She began to cry. "Mom this is what you did. You fell, Daddy too. I couldn't go get you."

I tried to explain to her, "Daddy and Mother had an accident. It was very smart of you, Véronique, not to come to pick us up. Instead, you got help. Darling, you did so well, you saved mommy."

It didn't matter what I told her. I could feel her pain. Every time that I would see a doll falling to the floor, my insides tightened into a knot. Véronique felt so much pain. I was unable to help my daughter without professional help.

Véronique cried everyday when it became dark outside. She began to complain about a rash on her body, but nothing was visible. She woke up each morning crying. She suffered from headaches regularly. I felt that all of her pain was created by stress because she had seen her father fall to his death in Angeles Crest Canyon.

Véronique was nervous too. She disliked everything I spoke of concerning her father. She was afraid of everything concerning her "daddy." She cried a lot.

I decided to call a counselor specializing in children, Antoinette Krell. We started to go there in April, 1983. During the first session, I was with Véronique. The counselor advised me to buy her a doll house about 30 inches high by 24 inches wide, which I did. Véronique put the house together herself. It came with a mama, papa, sister, and brother dolls, and a dog doll; a complete family. It was a two story house.

Antoinette told me, "Let her play with that as long as she wants, she'll probably make the dolls fall. Let her do it because it'll help her to empty her emotions. Right now she's reliving what she saw in the mountains when her father fell, then you fell too. It's important that you give her the freedom to do it."

I let Véronique play with that doll house and the dolls everyday. She would put papa doll on the edge of the roof and let it fall. She took mama doll in her hands, put her on the balcony, and let her fall. Every time that she would do that, I felt that I was falling. I was terrified, but I didn't have any choice. I let her do it. She never used the girl doll or boy doll to make them fall. It was only the parents. I asked her to let me play with her. We started to use the children dolls and the dog doll. We changed their bedrooms and redecorated their family room. As I recall, we played with the house and family dolls all summer. At the same time she was in psychotherapy. Three months of therapy was enough. Her desire to see the papa and mama dolls falling was gone.

Véronique would come back from the psychotherapy session and tell me, "Mama, Antoinette taught me how to make soup today." Then every day when we would play with the house together, she would say, "We'll also make soup."

Every Saturday, for the period of one year, I had a driver that came to my house and drove Véronique to Torrance to see her counselor. My daughter was finally coming out of her emotional trauma. Every Wednesday after school, my driver would drive her to the Karate Studio. Many times I would join Véronique. She did both psychotherapy and karate for a complete year.

After each psychotherapy session, she would come to tell me how daddy fell, and how I fell. Every week she had something new to tell me. It took twelve months, and today she's very healthy emotionally. The psychotherapy also cured the stomach pain that she had everyday following the accident. She finished her karate courses and earned a green belt. Relatively speaking, the time it took Véronique to complete the Karate course and psychotherapy treatments was very short. She was excellent in Karate. She just loved it.

Before Véronique started her psychotherapy treatments and karate courses, she was always asking me, "Mother, if we go to Korea, could we find my first daddy?" I told her that I wanted to go to Korea with her, but we could not find her first father. "We'll see your country and some day mama will get remarried. You'll have another daddy."

In the middle of March, 1983, when Véronique returned to her classes at Madrona Elementary School, I would drive her to school every morning and pick her up at three o'clock. Many students clustered around Véronique, questioning her about her father and mother, and the accident. They wanted to know how she felt about it. She completed the school year there. The school authorities and the parents of the students that were in the same class with Véronique were very kind. The students' parents would invite Véronique for dinner or to go to Disneyland or to the beach. Parents would visit me at my residence. Everyone was supporting my child for the balance of the year 1983, and Véronique obtained excellent grades. I was very grateful.

The following year, I was advised by Véronique's counselor to change her school. According to the counselor, Véronique's classmates were paying too much attention to the tragic accident. Véronique seemed happy to change schools. She liked the idea of new teachers, new friends, and no more talk about daddy's death and mom's comatose period. It became a clear field which allowed her to concentrate only on herself and her studies.

September of 1983, Véronique came home one day and told me, "Mother, I met a girlfriend at school. She's in my class and lives with her father.

"What's her name?"

"Gwen. We want you to meet her father, mom. They're like you and me. They're alone."

I agreed to meet him and Véronique's friend. So, Gwen's father, Don, invited us to go to Magic Mountain. I was unable to go to Magic Mountain, but Véronique spent the day with them. When they came back home, she invited Gwen to sleep over. The next day, which was Sunday, Don called to invite all of us for lunch. After that Don and I went out together for almost a year. Everyone was happy.

During this time, Véronique completed her psychotherapy sessions. Because I had a man in my life, Véronique felt safe. She would tell me, "Mother, I would like to have a daddy. I don't want to be adopted by another dad. I just want you to get married."

CHAPTER 9 - LIBIDO

By April of 1983, I thought that the most important parts of my life were in order. Véronique was doing well and my friend, Dustin, had returned to Canada. But I was still confused, and in pain. I decided to research what could be done for my brain damage and injuries. I had so much pain and mental confusion to deal with that I called 411 for the information operator and asked her for the name and address of a psychiatrist. I did not understand how medical referrals were handled in the United States.

The operator explained that she couldn't give me the name of a doctor, but she could give me the phone number of the hospital closest to where I live.

"Where do you live," she asked.

"I live in Thousand Oaks."

She gave me the phone number of the hospital and told me to call there and ask for a referral to a psychiatrist.

"They'll help you," she said.

The hospital receptionist gave me the name of Dr. Andreassen, whom I called and made an appointment with. The first week of that month, I started to see Dr. Andreassen. I explained to him how lost I was, emotionally, physically, and intellectually, since the accident and how much pain my body had. I explained to him how the injury happened.

Dr. Andreassen said, "Mrs. Kuhlman, you should ask your neurologist to give you a myelogram. *(A myelogram is like a spinal tap. Dye being flowed inside the spinal canal outlining the spinal cord itself. It allows the physician to see if there is a fracture.)* This way, if you have broken a vertebrae, your doctor will be able to see it." Upon my request, Dr. Andreassen referred me to a neurologist, Dr. Deegan.

When I called Dr. Deegan for an appointment, I was told I would have to wait until May 24th, 1983. I took the appointment date, but I was not going to wait two months to see a doctor and get treatment. I decided to look in the telephone book to see if I could find an orthopedist. Not one was listed, so I called the hospital again to get another referral. The receptionist gave me a few telephone numbers and doctors' names. I called an orthopedist, Dr. Sapiro, and was able to make an appointment for April 18th, 1983.

When I went to his office, Dr. Sapiro examined me. He explained that the movements of my legs, arms, and neck were normal.

"There is a mark in the lumbar part of your back. Did you ever have back surgery?" he asked.

"In 1970, I had lumbar fifth disc herniation surgery done," I answered.

"The pain is probably coming from that surgery," Dr. Sapiro said.

"But this is 1983. Thirteen years have gone by since my back surgery, and I never had pain there before my accident."

"We'll take X-rays," he said, "And see what they show."

After all the X-rays were complete, Dr. Sapiro told me everything looked good. "Maybe the pain is a result of your brain damage."

One month later, I kept my appointment with Dr. Deegan, the neurologist. Again, I explained the physical pain that I had, and told him that my psychiatrist had advised me to talk to him about having a myelogram.

Dr. Deegan said, "I'll have you take X-rays to see what is wrong . . . what it shows. I'll give you a prescription for pain pills. When I get the results, I'll call you to let you know."

I went to the hospital to have X-rays taken and then to the drug store to fill the prescription. I took the pills until the bottle was empty. Three days after I took the X-rays, Dr. Deegan called at my home to inform me that he had the results and they were good. Everything was normal. He didn't know why I had so much pain and difficulty walking.

"Would you let me take a myelogram?" I asked. "I'm still having pain."

"I would have recommended a myelogram if the X-rays had shown some problems. But, everything looks fine. A myelogram is too serious an exam to have when it's not necessary," he said.

"Dr. Deegan, I have pain. This test is necessary."

"Let me give you one more prescription, Mrs. Kuhlman. Which drug store can I call for you?" (I had a bottle of pills in my purse so it was easy for me to give him the number.) The pills were delivered to my home and I took these pills until the bottle was empty. This was the second time that doctors dismissed my complaints, but I put my total trust in them and was in no condition to do otherwise at the time.

The following week at the psychiatrist's office, I told him that I had seen the neurologist, and he thought the pain was from the brain injury. He had told me, "When you have a brain injury, it's normal for your body to have pain everywhere."

"The pain isn't in your mind," Dr. Andreassen said. "You're very well in touch with your emotions. Insist on having a myelogram." He left it there, not aware that in my confused state, I was unable to insist on anything.

"I'll see you next week at the same time," Dr. Andreassen dismissed me, "I think you'll have to learn how to live with brain damage. Be sure to call your neurologist back."

I became so desperate, I looked everywhere I could to get help for what I was going through. One of my friends took me to St. Patrick's Catholic Church in Thousand Oaks to see a priest. No one told me about pain management clinics where they help people in my situation.

At St. Patrick's Church, I was so distraught, I told the priest that I wanted to see John again. I wanted to take care of my daughter all by myself like I always did, drive her to school, cook for her, help her with her homework, go horseback riding with her. My questions to the priest were like those to the psychiatrists. Why did I lose everything? Why did this happen to me? I didn't hurt anybody. There are people that rape and kill every day, and they don't get punished for the bad things they're doing. God doesn't punish them. I just wanted to save my husband's life, and I lost everything. Why was God punishing me? The priest tried to console me.

I felt like my head was full of water. It was now May of 1983. Whenever I would stand up, I became dizzy. I felt helpless, not knowing what I should do next.

At the time I didn't know why I had so many physical injuries, so much pain. Was it in my mind? I constantly tried to imagine how high 600 feet is. I looked for answers for years. Today, I realize that my fall was severe enough to destroy my complete body. Before my brain stabilized, I desperately needed answers. Were my difficulties caused by the coma I was in, and could they someday be relieved, or was my brain damage permanent?

I explained to all the medical doctors the problems I was having. I couldn't drive, therefore, I was forced to depend on a driver; I had problems with some members of my family; and, my deceased husband's health insurance company was denying coverage on several of my medical bills. In addition, everyday living was a constant struggle. I had forgotten how to cook, and I could no longer taste food. It didn't matter what I put in my mouth, there was no taste. I had lost that sense. My daughter would say, "Put some spice in, Mom." I didn't have any idea what a spice was. Life was very difficult.

I felt very insecure and alone. I needed to be loved all the time, but I didn't understand why. I was always dizzy and had difficulty walking. I was only able to write by sound, I couldn't recognize people that I had apparently known for years, and I had lost my ability to use a computer, adding machine, typewriter, VCR, or any modern machine.

I had to relearn my age, every part of my body, how to sit down and stand. I also had to completely learn about my daughter, Véronique's life. After raising a child for seven years, you never think that some day you'll be in a situation where you have to relearn what you taught her since she was born. Now, I had to learn from her even though she was only seven years of age.

When I told my friend and driver, Arlene, what was happening with my doctors, that they could not see the problems I had with pain, she recommended that I see a chiropractor.

"I know one in Ventura," she said. "He is very good. Let me call him for you."

Not knowing what else to do, I made an appointment with the chiropractor in July, 1983. He listened to the story of the accident and my 600-foot fall. Then he put me in a room, made me lie down on a table and started to adjust me. He also pushed on my back. After 4 visits, my pain had not diminished. I was unable to sit down, and had many more problems standing up and walking.

"I believe that you should see a neurologist. I can always give you more treatments, but I don't know if it will help," he said. I thanked him and left, feeling very frustrated and not knowing where to turn.

I got another referral from the hospital for a neurologist, Dr. Sherwood. I went to see him, explained how I got injured and how I had great pain resulting from the fall. He took more X-rays, prescribed more pills, and finally told me that after a brain injury, it was normal for my body to have so much pain. The X-ray results were normal. He subtly suggested that I would just have to learn to live with it. I saw Dr. Sherwood a few more times and got treatment and prescription pills, but nothing helped.

No other person could see or measure the pain I had. Because I looked physically healthy, people didn't realize that I could be suffering from internal fractures. The X-rays showed nothing wrong. The doctors I saw were so limited concerning physical pain. They all suggested it was just in my mind, a result of my brain injury. If relief from pain is ignored, there can be tragic unnecessary consequences. Even with medications my doctors' prescribed, the degree of my pain would not change.

I tried so many times to tell my doctors that I wasn't suffering from chronic pain. (I use their term, "chronic pain," even if I dislike these two words). For some reason, these doctors couldn't realize or refused to see, or were unable to understand. The pain could be treated if the medical doctors would administer appropriate treatment. It could be done through surgery, physical therapy, or occupational therapy. Proper medical treatment could release me from that pain. I thought, "If I can only meet a medical doctor that knows what he is doing."

When you suffer from brain damage, family members, friends, medical doctors, and even some lawyers think that you are mentally disturbed. The physical pain you say you have is all in your mind, according to them.

It was extremely difficult for me, at the time just after my fall, to explain where I hurt, where I might possibly have fractures internally. I just knew that I was in pain. Where was it coming from? After seeing the neurologists, the orthopedist, a chiropractor and a psychiatrist, I felt the only one that could understand me was the psychiatrist.

I decided to see Dr. Andreassen, a neuropsychiatrist, three times a week in Thousand Oaks, and Dr. Krell, a psychiatrist, once a week in Torrance. When the weekends would come, I was sad, because I so much needed their support and help to teach me how to handle the new life I was facing.

From the time Dustin left, my girlfriends, Shannon and Ariel, would come to see me at home everyday. Shannon was upset, seeing me confined to my bed because of physical pain, and one day asked, "Why don't you go see Dr. Cucumb again?"

"Who is he?" I asked.

"He's the doctor who took care of you at the emergency room, and in intensive care when you were in the hospital right after they found you in the mountains."

"I can't remember anyone who took care of me in California after my accident."

"Let me find the phone number and address for you. I have it at home because I called there every day. I went to see you often. You can call and make an appointment with him."

After returning home, Shannon gave me the information and I called Dr. Cucumb's office. The secretary gave me an appointment for July 26th. I explained to Dr. Cucumb how dizzy I was and how much pain I had in my right leg, back, right arm, hand, finger, shoulder, right side of my neck, and in my face. I poured out my fears and confusion. I told him that I felt I was in a little box. My body didn't have any place to move, and I felt like my spirit was in a full drawer with no space available. I had a tremendous job to do to recover, find space for my legs to stretch, my arms, my body, my toes, to focus my eyes, and to mend my ears.

Every part of my body needed to find its own place, and its function.

My spirit felt lost. My life functions were like a drawer of software. The brain software that hadn't been erased was all mixed up. The software that was damaged wanted to come back. That was why I felt I needed so many psychiatrists and psychologists. How was I supposed to handle these things?

At my first appointment, I asked Dr. Cucumb how he became my doctor.

"I was working at the emergency hospital the day of your accident, and Kyung Ok Hospital was the only hospital in the area that had helicopters. I went with the helicopter rescue team to rescue you from the canyon."

"I guess I'm lucky to have had you as my doctor when I fell

The next few pages illustrate the brain
power that a child brings to our life.

The author, Odette-Marie, at age 3 with her family.
Bottom row, third from the left.

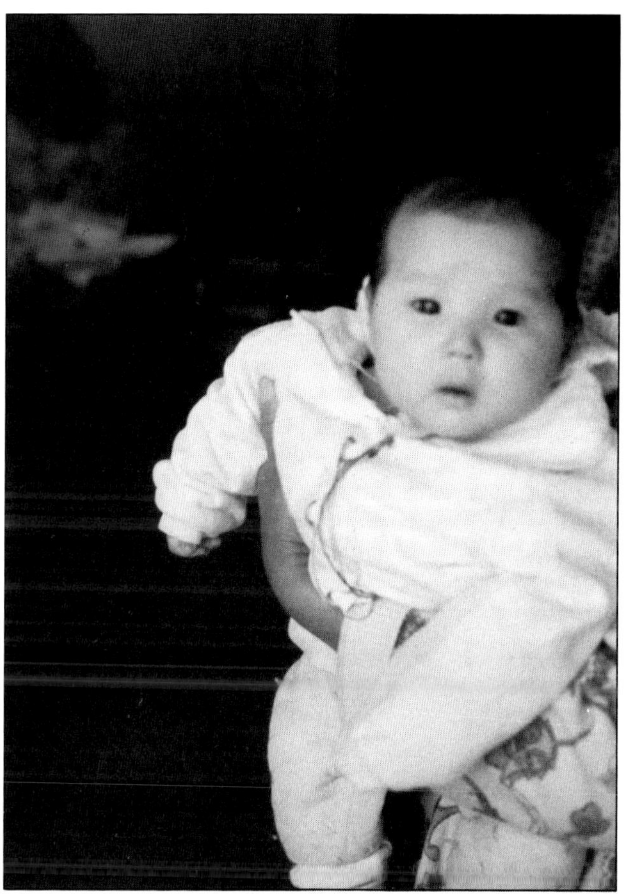

Picture of 2½ month old child that we received from Seoul, Korea. John and I decided to adopt this beautiful baby girl just by looking at her picture.

*Her arrival in Dorval International Airport.
Our little princess that we had decided to
name Odette Véronique had arrived to her
new country, Canada.*

*John holding his 5½
month old daughter.
I am admiring her cute
dress that she was
wearing on her arrival.*

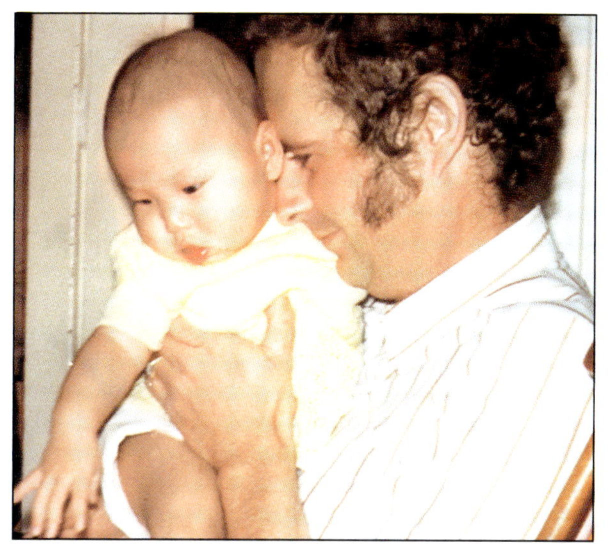

Odette Véronique in her Dad's arms at our home in Québec. She was 6 months old.

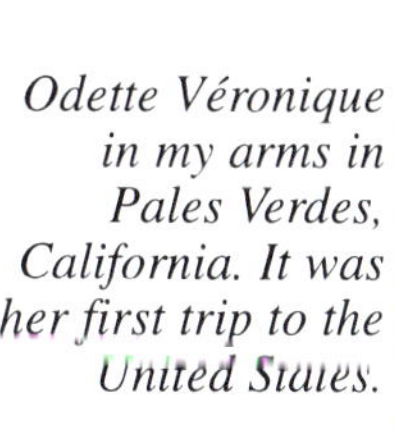

Odette Véronique in my arms in Pales Verdes, California. It was her first trip to the United States.

Time for a refill!

Easter 1979 at my parents-in-law, Pales Verdes.
My mother-in-law, John and her first grandchild.

*John, Odette Véronique and Césars, 1976
in our new home, Thousand Oaks,
California.*

*Odette Véronique
Romper Room, a television program
December 1981 Hollywood, California*

A month before John's death, hiking with our daughter.

*1982, Odette Véronique in the San
Bernardino mountains.*

1983 Karate in progress for Odette Véronique

Véronique's graduation picture

Members of the San Dimas Mountain and Sylmar Mountain rescue teams carry out the body of 37-year-old John Kuhlman of Chatsworth from a snowy gorge in the Angeles National Forest Tuesday morning after a 22-hour search for the victim. His wife, Odette Kuhlman, of Newbury Park, was hospitalized in serious, but stable condition. (AP photo)

The author, Odette Marie's brain after the 600 Foot Fall. Frontal lobe brain damage.

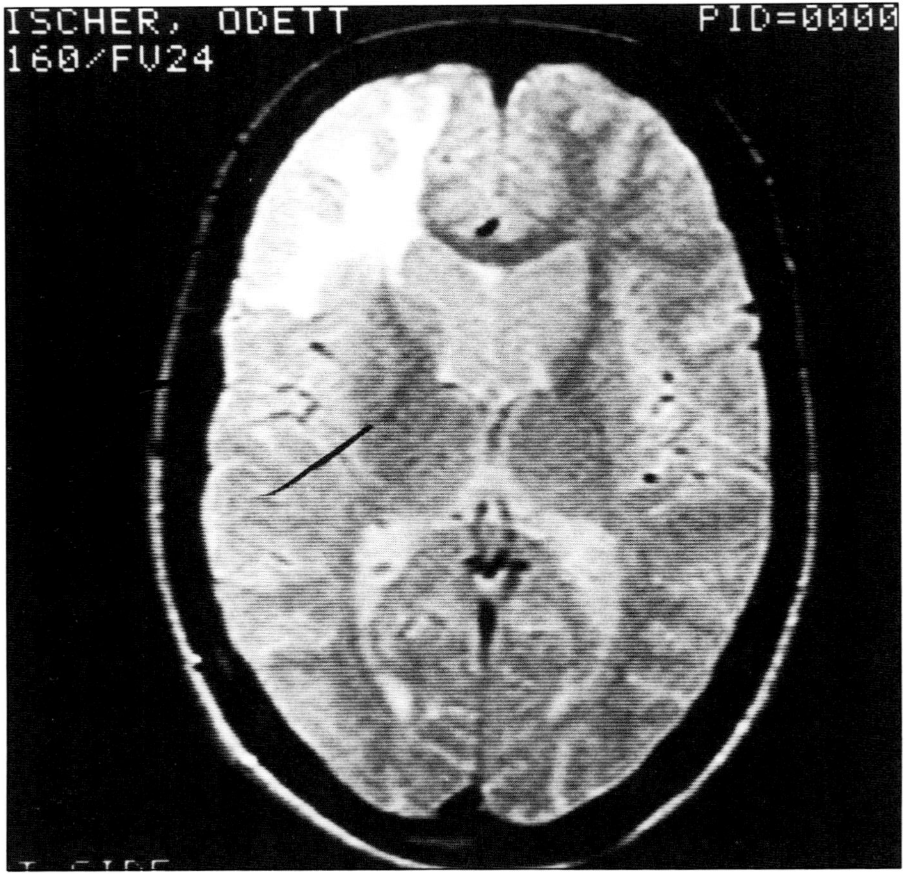

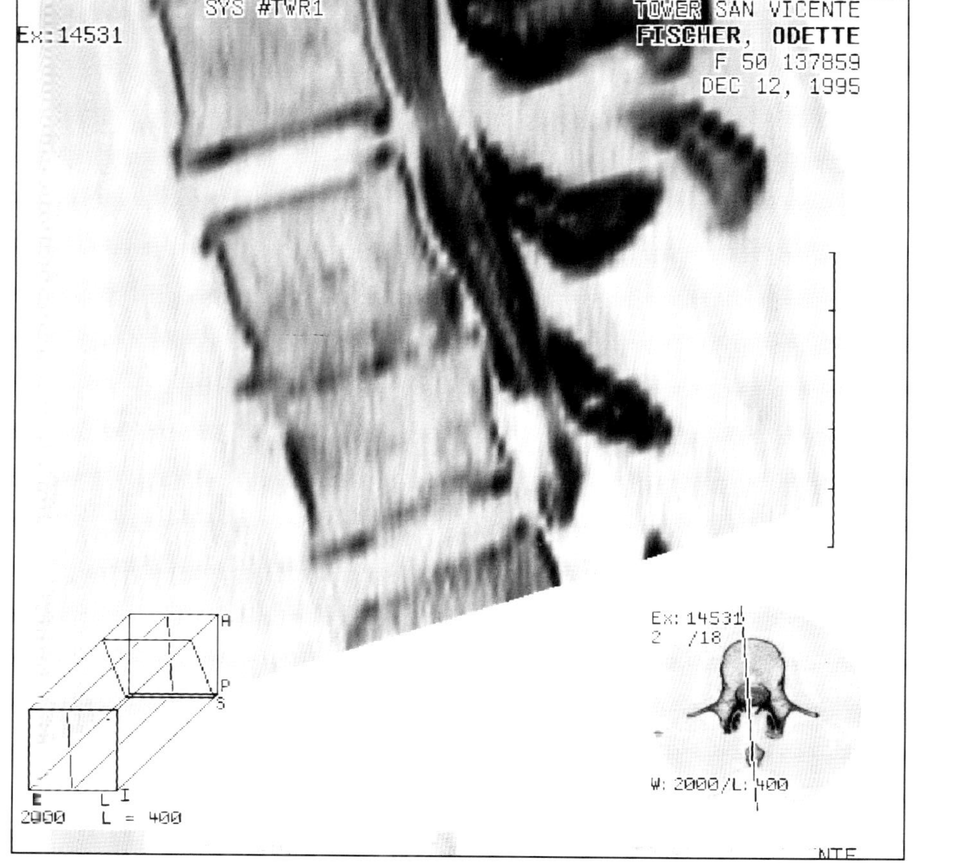

Odette Marie's spinal cord. Overgrowth of bone from the fusion.

The author, Odette Marie, December 1982.

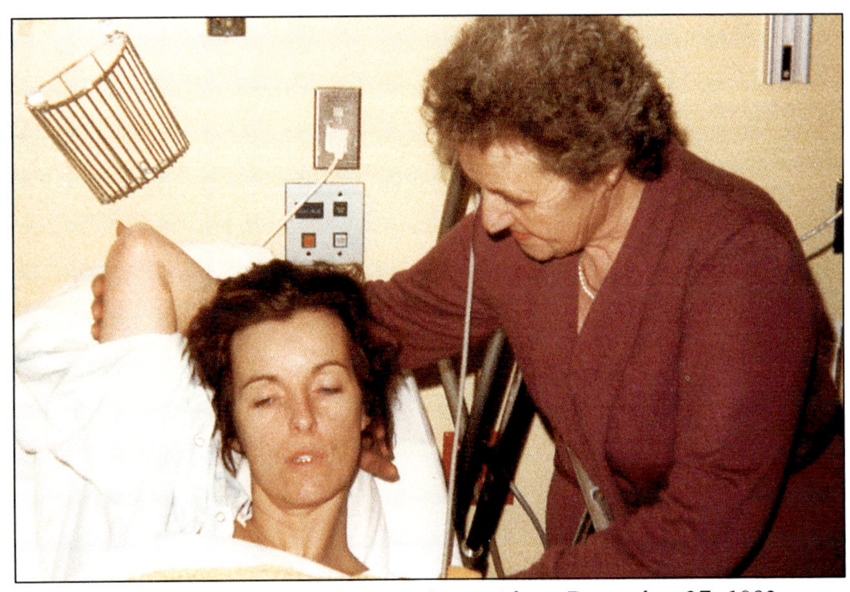

The author several hours after the accident, December 27, 1982.

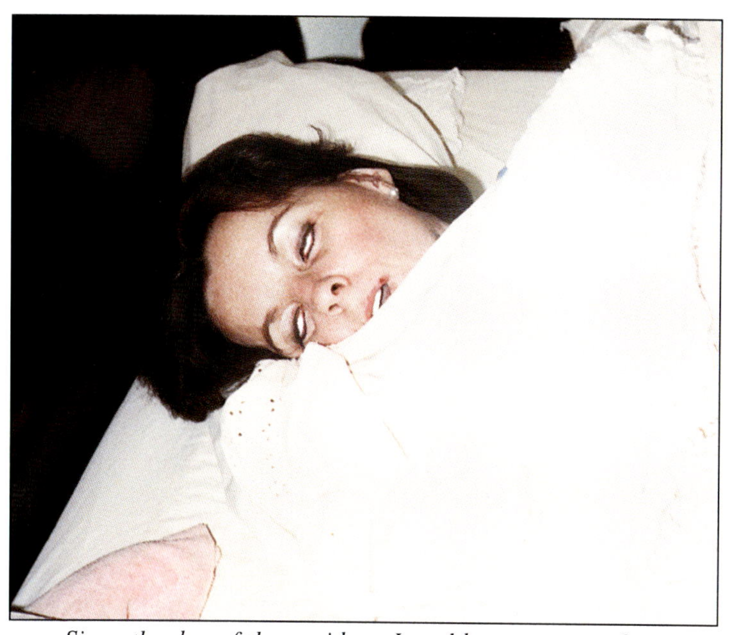

Since the day of the accident, I could not open or close my eyes completely . . . And no physician to help me.

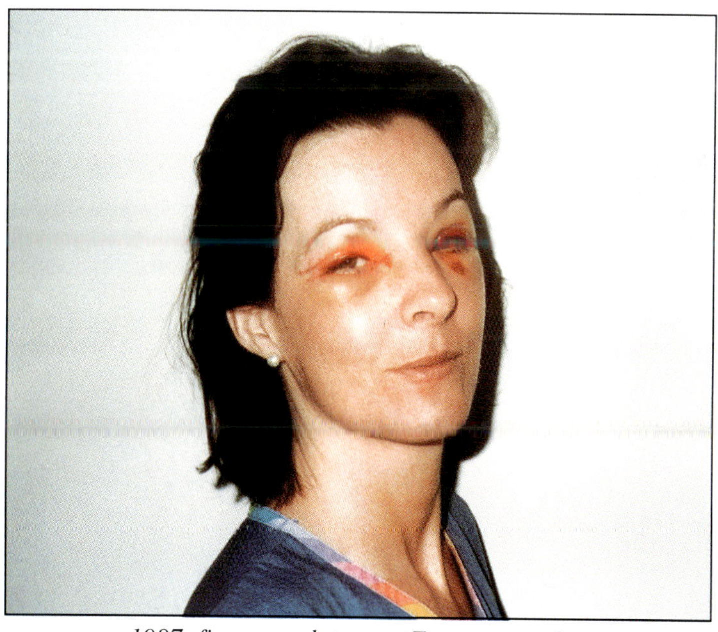

1987, five years later . . . Eye surgery that made my vision worse.

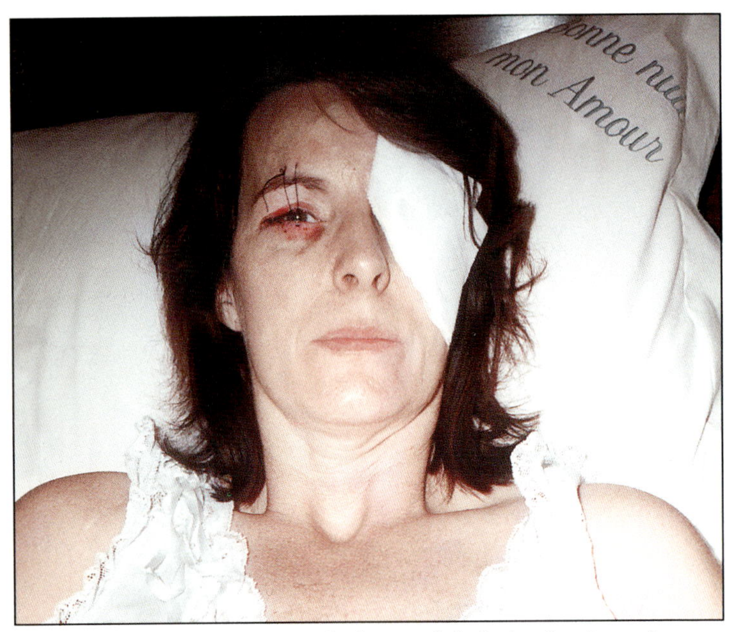

It took me 9 years to find an ophthalmic plastic and reconstructive surgeon that could help.

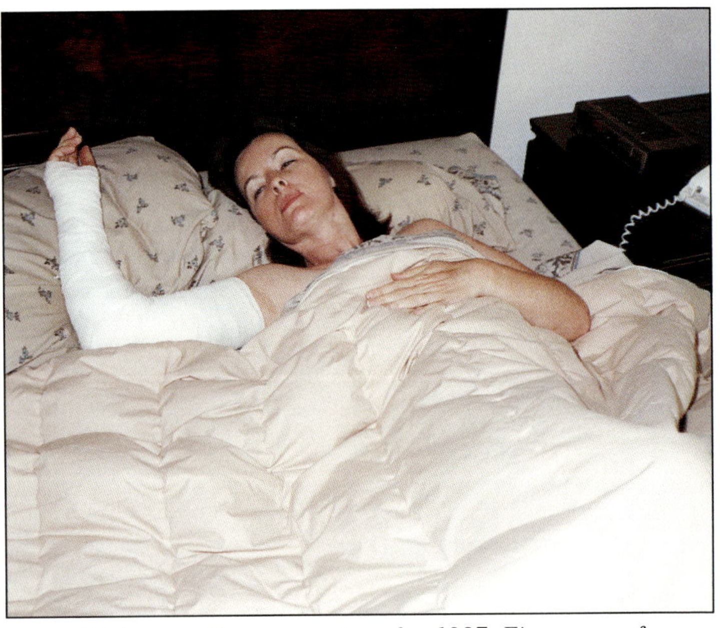

Right arm Ulnar nerve transfer, 1987. Five years of research to find the proper neurologist and orthopedist.

down 600 feet. Without you, I would probably have died."

"Mrs. Kuhlman, you were lucky to have been found at the time by the rescue team. When I saw you, at the moment I touched your arm, you went into a coma."

He asked if I remembered anything from my time in the Kyung Ok Hospital. "Do you see your family?"

"No, they're all in Canada. I'm the only one outside the country. I don't speak to my brother and sisters who came here when I was comatose."

"In the history of the hospital, we never saw a person like your sister. We couldn't believe that she existed. It was like in a movie. To see someone so disturbed. We had to call the hospital guard to keep her quiet."

"Which one was giving you problems? Apparently two of my sisters came here."

"I don't know her name. I know that she was heavy."

"What was she doing?" I asked.

"She argued with everyone that would come to see you."

"That was my sister, Simone."

"Your sister wanted to control everybody. Nurses and doctors could not believe what she was doing. She wasn't acting like a human being. You were in intensive care, comatose. It was extremely important for you as a patient to be kept calm. You were in a serious condition, but with your sister there, it was impossible."

After listening to what Dr. Cucumb had to tell me regarding some members of my family, I apologized for Simone creating so many problems. I explained to him that Simone and my mother had filed a lawsuit against the State of California because of the accident.

Dr. Cucumb responded, "If your lawyer needs me as a witness, tell him to call me . . . I'll say what he wants me to say in court."

I explained then about my fear, my insecurity. "Something is wrong in me. For some reason, I feel the need to be loved all the time. This isn't me. I feel that I'm in a different body. It wasn't like that before."

"After a brain injury, this is normal, Mrs. Kuhlman," he said. "You could have become a lesbian or a libido. You're lucky. You're a libido."

"What does it mean?" I asked.

"A high libido person always has sexual desires," Dr. Cucumb told me.

"How long am I going to be like that?" I was shocked. "Probably all your life," Dr. Cucumb said. "But you're very lucky. The man that will be with you will be very happy. You'll always be able to give him love. You are never going to become tired of it."

"That is too much," I gasped. "I can't take this. My husband is dead. I don't have any man. Please write down on a piece of paper this word that you just told me. I must look in the dictionary and see exactly what is happening to me."

Dr. Cucumb took a piece of paper, and wrote down, *"LIBIDO."* He added verbally, "In our brain, we have a part for sex, a part for study and analyzing, a part for taste, etc. In your case, your brain damage caused injuries to the sexual part of your brain. You can't do anything about it. Just accept it."

He gave me a prescription, and told me to make an appointment for August 18th, 1983. But before I left his office, he asked me, "Do you live alone?"

"During the summer, my daughter is at the Bar 717 camp in Northern California. During that time, I live by myself."

I left his office. Arlene was waiting for me in the waiting room.

We went to the drug store for the pain pills, and she drove me home.

The next day, my friend Susan was visiting in the afternoon. She was like Shannon, always checking on me. We were in the front room talking when the telephone rang. I answered.

"Mrs. Kuhlman, I'd like to see you, this is Dr. Cucumb speaking."

"Who?" I asked. My recall was still not good.

"Dr. Cucumb, the doctor that took care of you when you were in the coma. I also saw you yesterday at my office. I'd like to see how you are."

"When would you like to see me?"

"Now. Are you alone?" he asked me.

"No, my girlfriend is with me. But, come over if you want."

"No, No." he said. "When is she going to leave?"

"I don't know, but just come over, it doesn't matter if she's here."

"I want to see you alone. Can you ask her to leave?"

"She'll be leaving in about thirty minutes."

"That's too long."

"Where are you?" I asked.

"I'm in my car in front of your home."

"How can you call me if you are in your car?" I said.

"I have a telephone in my car. Please ask your friend to leave now."

"Just one minute, I'm going to ask her." I looked at Susan, and told her that Dr. Cucumb was in his car and wanted to come to see me, but he wanted to see me alone.

"Can you leave?" I asked.

"Yes. I'm leaving."

I picked up the telephone and told Dr. Cucumb that Susan would be leaving in five minutes.

"Fine," he said, What color are her clothes? I want to be sure that she is gone."

I described Susan and her clothes to Dr. Cucumb and then hung up the telephone.

"What's happening?" Susan asked.

"I don't have any idea. I met this doctor yesterday in his office, and now, he's at my home. I don't know. He told me that he was in his car at the door. Why don't you check to see if it's true? I didn't give him my address, nor my telephone number. How did he find me?"

Susan said, "I don't know, but I'm leaving. I'll talk to you later." She hurried to leave.

Immediately after Susan had left my home, Dr. Cucumb was at the door. I invited him into the living room and asked what he wanted.

He said, "You shouldn't be standing up, you should be in bed with the pain you have in your back, and right leg. Where is your bedroom?"

I showed him the stairs, and said, "My bedroom is the white room."

He said, "Let me put you to bed."

"I can't remove my clothes in front of you," I said.

"Why not?" he asked.

"I'm not going to be without clothes in front of you."

"I won't look at you. Just get undressed, I'll close my eyes."

"If you want me to take off my clothes, go out of my bedroom."

He accepted that and went out into the hall. I removed my clothes, put my night dress on, got in bed and covered myself with the blanket. I was confused, but felt I should do what my doctor was telling me.

A little bit later, he came back in my bedroom, took off his clothes and got in my bed.

"What are you doing?" I asked. "Why are you coming in my bed?"

"I'm not going to hurt you. I just want to talk with you."

"Dr. Cucumb, I don't want you in my bed. We can talk downstairs."

"I want to show you what you were doing to me when you came out of your coma."

I looked at his face. I was lost. I didn't know what to do nor what to tell him. Why was he doing this?

"Why aren't you at your office with your patients?" I asked. Somehow I knew this was not right. I was very confused.

"Are you married? Do you have children?"

"Yes," he answered. "I'm married. I have two children with my first wife, a son and a daughter, and my second wife is pregnant. Wait just a minute. I have to call my office." He turned his body toward the night table and made his phone call, saying, "I'm at the hospital in the emergency room right now. I'll be at the office soon." Then he hung up.

He turned back toward me and said, "When you came out of the coma, I was close to your bed. You touched my penis. You were caressing me. I asked the nurse and your family to leave me alone with you."

He took my hand, controlling it. I was paralyzed emotionally and physically by what he was doing. I couldn't speak. I didn't understand what Dr. Cucumb wanted.

He said, "You're alone in California. You can depend on me. If you need something, day or night, call me. I'll tell my answering service and receptionist to accept all your calls."

Then he started to touch my body. He kissed me, telling me how beautiful I was, and he said that he would always take care of me. I wouldn't have to worry about anything.

"What about your wife? What would she say about this?"

"She won't know. I can take care of you and her at the same time. If you call on the weekend, the service will transfer your phone call to my home. If my wife answers, just ask for me. Don't speak to her about anything."

"Why are you touching me?"

"I must teach you how to make love. It's important for your brain to regain what it lost. I'm not going to hurt you. I'm going to do everything, you don't have to touch me. If you have pain, tell me."

I stared at this doctor, not knowing how to think, nor what to think. My mental faculties weren't in complete working order. I was like a baby of seven months old in my second life. The only difference was my body. I had the body of a woman of thirty-seven years, but, my spirit/brain was just reborn. It was a beginning, my second life.

"Do you remember what your husband did when he made love to you?" Dr. Cucumb asked.

"I can't remember my husband. How can I remember how he made love."

"Okay, don't speak. Let me teach you. Just do what I tell you to do. Touch my hair. When I kiss you, you kiss me."

He said sentences like that for a while, kissing my body, putting my breast in his mouth. After that, he said how good I tasted and that he wanted to be with me all the time.

A few minutes later, he said, "Put your legs around my waist."

"What do you mean?" I asked.

He answered and showed me, "Here around my body."

"You want to put my legs there? But I want to keep the blanket on me."

"I'll keep the blanket on my back, he said, so you'll be covered." He added, "You see how hard I am?"

"What are you talking about?"

"When I came to your bed, my penis was small. I'm excited now that I've touched you. I desire you. My penis is now longer and bigger. Now, stop asking questions and put your legs around my body like I showed you. Let me do what I want."

I was quiet. He moved his body on me. "I'm inside you. My penis is in your vagina," he said.

A few minutes later, he said, "I'm coming."

"Where are you going?" I asked.

"Don't you know what it means when I say I'm coming? Your husband never told you that when he made love to you?" Dr. Cucumb asked.

"I don't know. I've never heard these words before."

"I'll explain it to you later," he told me. After a while, he asked me to go with him to the bathroom.

"I don't want you to see me without my clothes," I said. I kept my night dress on me all the time when I was in bed.

"Odette Marie, come with me to the bathroom. I've seen undressed women before. I'm married. I'm a doctor, I see people undress all the time in the hospital and I just made love to you. Come with me in the shower."

He went to the bathroom, started the shower, and asked me for some towels. I told him where they were and he went to get them.

When he returned he said, "I want you to take your shower with me."

"I'll take my shower later."

"It's too dangerous, you may fall," he said. "I want you to come in the shower with me right now."

I went with him to the bathroom and said, "You go first. When you're in, I'll go also. I have to remove my night dress."

"Okay, I'm going in the shower."

Once he was in, I took off my night dress and got in too.

When we had finished and put our clothes on, Dr. Cucumb looked at me and said, "Don't tell anybody what we did together. This is between you and me. It's our secret. If you need something, you call me."

He picked up the telephone, dialed a number and spoke, "This is Dr. Cucumb speaking. I'll be at the office in thirty minutes. If there are any messages, put them on my desk."

Then he left my home.

That evening, when Susan called me to find out what Dr. Cucumb wanted, I told her what he wanted to teach me and what I had done to him when I came out of the coma. I also told her that he got in bed with me. I explained that he didn't want me to stand up, because of my back and leg pain. He said that I must be in bed.

"I have so much pain, I did what he wanted," I told Susan. "He said that he would always protect me, and that I can call him at any time." I told her that I explained to Dr. Cucumb how afraid I was of being paralyzed because of the pain in my leg and back. Dr. Cucumb had answered me, "I didn't let you die on the mountain, and I won't let you become paralyzed. It's important for your brain that I teach you how to make love."

Susan couldn't believe that a doctor would drive forty-five miles to make love to his patient. She said that it was a bad thing that he had done, and asked me if he was going to come back to my house.

"I don't know," I said.

"He may be your medical doctor since your accident and he knows how injured you are, but what he is doing to you isn't professional. Odette Marie, tomorrow I'll come to talk to you about it."

"But Dr. Cucumb is a security for me." I said. "He'll not let me become paralyzed. If I need any treatment, he said that he'll take care of me. Susan, I have nobody to protect me. I don't know why he is doing this. He said that when I was in the coma, he thought that I was a beautiful woman. At that time, he desired me.

"I'll see you tomorrow," Susan said. Then she hung up.

For weeks afterward, Dr. Cucumb came to my home without asking me first. He would call when he was already parked in front of my house. He drove forty-five miles to come to Thousand Oaks to make love to me, and to promise that he would always take care of me. He made me feel secure. Nothing bad would happen to my body, because according to him, he would always be there to help me.

CHAPTER 10 - DOCTORS

Every time that Dr. Cucumb would come to my home, I would tell him how dizzy I was. I didn't know why I was feeling dizzy. Even when I was in bed, lying on my back, I saw the room turning. When I changed from the right side of my body to the left, everything would turn.When I stood up, I had to hold on to something for balance. I did drive my car occasionally because I needed to prove to myself that I was still able to do it.

One morning I decided to drive to Coldwell Banker Residential Real Estate office. Prior to my accident in 1980/1981, I had worked there and liked the people in my office. I was on Thousand Oaks Boulevard when a policeman stopped me and asked for my registration and driver's license. He told me I would have to get out of the car and pass a drunk driving test.

"What have you had to drink?"

"I drank water," I said.

"Put your hands on the car, you must pass this test now."

I did what he wanted me to do, the result showing that I had no alcohol in my body.

"You were driving on Thousand Oaks Boulevard on both sides of the double line. You must keep on your right side, otherwise you're going to kill yourself, and kill or hurt someone else."

I told the policeman that I never drink alcohol. I explained that my dizziness was because of the accident, and told him I suffered from brain damage.

It doesn't matter," he said. "I'm going to give you a ticket. I can't let you drive like that. You can explain it to the judge."

I opened my notebook (agenda) and gave the policeman the name and telephone number of Doctor Cucumb, asking him to call.

"Dr. Cucumb will certify what I just told you about the Canyon accident."

The policeman refused.

I didn't have to pay the ticket because Dr. Cucumb wrote a letter to the judge explaining my situation. After that I didn't drive the car by myself. My driver and friend, Arlene, would take me to my doctor appointments.

At that time Dr. Cucumb decided to refer me to an ear specialist, Dr. Grate. "Don't tell Dr. Grate what we have been doing together. Don't talk about me being at your home," he warned. On October 3rd, 1983, I saw Dr. Grate for the first time. After discussing my symptoms, he decided to have me take an inner ear test. I took the test on October 11th, 1983, which made me very sick. Dr. Grate said, "You need inner ear surgery. Your ear is perforated. This is why you're so dizzy. Furthermore, you're not allowed to drive an automobile until the surgery is done."

The inner ear surgery was done October 17th, 1983. Dr. Grate took skin from behind my ear and plugged the inner ear hole of my right ear. I hoped it would solve my balance problem. But eight days later, when my driver took me back to Dr. Grate for a check up, I was still experiencing dizziness; not as much, but it was still there. I continued to see the ear doctor for a while. According to

Dr. Grate, time would help cure the dizziness.

When you are stubborn and determined, sometimes it can create problems. I had one more appointment with the ear surgeon on November 21st, 1983. It was a follow-up to see if the inner ear was well plugged. I still had a great need to prove to myself that I could be independent again, so I decided to drive there myself. After all, the ear had been repaired, I should have no difficulty. The doctor's office was located thirty-seven miles from my house. I left home at nine o'clock in the morning and had no problem driving there. I was extremely proud of myself. Dr. Grate made me take a test to check the inner ear. My dizziness became so severe, everything around me was turning. I couldn't stay seated or walk. The nurse made me lie down. Dr. Grate told me that the inner ear was well plugged, but since the surgery was done only a month ago, the dizziness would continue and then diminish with time. He was concerned that it was so severe.

"Your driver will have to drive you home," Dr. Grate said. "I'll give you a prescription. Take the medication and don't do much for a while.""I drove myself this morning," I said. "I wanted to do it alone. I didn't tell my driver that I was coming here."

"Give me the name of your driver and the telephone number where I can reach her," Dr. Grate was concerned. "She has to come to pick you up. I can't let you drive your car."

I gave Dr. Grate the telephone number of Coldwell Banker Residential Real Estate, where Arlene worked. The nurse called and spoke with Arlene. She showed up with Pat to pick me up in the afternoon. Arlene took me home, and Pat drove my car to the office. I apologized for creating so many problems. That was the last time I drove my car alone for over three years.

The doctor explained that the ear surgery would not fix all my problems with dizziness, only the part affected by the inner ear. The head trauma also created dizziness and unbalance.

Following the inner ear surgery, the next step was to find a solution for my back pain, and my right leg and foot pain. Everyday it grew worse. I stayed in bed most of the day, took the pills I was prescribed, but nothing changed. The pain was persistent.

Dr. Cucumb recommended that I try a hot pad. Since I didn't know what he was talking about, he asked me to have Arlene call him. "I'll tell her to go to the drug store to buy you one."

When I called Arlene, she wasn't available, so another friend, John, who was an attorney, called Dr. Cucumb and secured a heating pad for me. "She should keep her back very warm and put pillows under her legs. Her back must be flat on the mattress," Dr. Cucumb said. Even though I followed the doctor's advice, my pain remained persistent.

Dr. Cucumb also sent me to Kyung Ok Hospital for a myelogram on November 6th, 1983. After receiving the results of the test, he referred me to Dr. Whits, an orthopedist, for a second opinion. In November of 1983, Dr. Cucumb examined the results of tests which had been sent to him. He recommended back surgery, a procedure called Fusion/Laminectomy, be done to the right and left side of my back. My sciatic nerve was injured due to herniation of the lumbar disk, and broken vertebrae.

On November 23rd, 1983, I saw Dr. Cucumb at his office. He informed me that because of the injured sciatic nerve, there was a ninety percent chance of being paralyzed following the surgery. "I've never seen a back so injured. You're lucky to be alive. Dr. Maker, an orthopedic surgeon, will join me to do the surgery. I'll do everything in my power to make sure that you don't lose the capacity to walk, but there is no guarantee. If we don't do the surgery, you'll probably become paralyzed anyway," he said.

He explained that the bones of my back were hurting the sciatic nerve, which goes from your brain to your toes. The surgery was absolutely necessary. I listened to what Dr. Cucumb had to tell me.

"What choice do I have?" I said. "Are you telling me that if I get the surgery done, I might wake up paralyzed?"

"Yes, that is what I'm telling you," Dr. Cucumb said. "I really can't know the results until the surgery is done. The sciatic nerve is seriously injured."

"If I don't get the surgery done, is it certain that I'll become paralyzed or be confined to my bed for the remainder of my life?"

Again the answer was, *yes*. "At the hospital the nurse will have you sign a release form stating that you have been made aware of the danger of the surgery. The hospital and medical doctors aren't held responsible if you become paralyzed."

"I don't have any choice," I said. "I'm unable to walk anyhow. My life depends on you one more time."

"Would you come to talk to me before they put me to sleep? I'm so afraid. My future is in your hands."

"Yes, I'll come to the hospital early," Dr. Cucumb said. "Don't worry. I won't let them put you to sleep until I talk with you. And, when you wake up, I'll be there beside you."

I was hospitalized on November 29th, 1983. While I waited, I called friends, asking them to pray for me. I also called my mother in Canada and told her how afraid I was. I didn't want to be paralyzed like my grand-mama Bégin had been. I asked mama to pray for me. "Only God and papa can keep me on my two legs," I said. Inside I was crying I was so afraid.

Mama told me, "Odette Marie, I'll call Colette and ask her to pray for you. Don't worry, you are going to be fine. Papa and God will help you. I've prayed for you everyday. Grand-mama Bégin was paralyzed but not for the same reason. She was paralyzed after eating a meal. We'll all pray for you."

My Grandmother Bégin had suffered from high blood pressure. One night at dinner she ate Creton (Pork Pate) and then went to work in the garden. When she bent down to pick vegetables, she suffered what was probably a minor stroke and became paralyzed on the right side of her body. I was terrified that the same thing could happen to me. I signed the release form for the protection of the doctors and hospital early the next morning. Then I called mama back.

"Colette, Germaine, Ruth and I are all together praying for you," she said. "Get the surgery done, I'll call you later during the day. Papa is there helping you. You're not alone. Don't be afraid," she said. I thanked mama and hung up the telephone. A few minutes later the nurse came in to give me a shot. She brought a stretcher to take me to a room closer to the surgery room.

"Where is Dr. Cucumb?" I asked.

"He'll be in to see you in a few minutes," she said.

I waited . . . so terrified. Dr. Cucumb arrived and told me he would do everything he could to make sure that I wouldn't be paralyzed. He kissed me and said, "Don't worry.When you wake up, I'll be there, holding your hand."

I woke up to Dr. Cucumb, his face looking down at me. "Everything went fine," he said. "It took us three hours to do the surgery. But, you're going to be well."

The second week that I was in the hospital, I told Dr. Cucumb that I wanted to see a psychiatrist.

"You don't need to see one," he said. "I'm here with you. I'm also a psychiatrist."

"You're not a psychiatrist, you're a neurosurgeon," I said.

"To become a neurologist you have to be a psychiatrist first. Tell me what is bothering you."

"No, I want to see a psychiatrist who practices here." Dr. Cucumb refused to let me see one.

My hospital stay lasted three weeks. The second week, Dr. Cucumb told me during his visit in the morning, "Odette Marie, you'll have to wear a brace for three to four months. The only time you'll remove it will be when you take your shower. Tomorrow, the man that will fit you for the brace will come to see you to take the measurements. I'll also be here."

The next day, the orthotist (bodycast technician) came to see me with Dr. Cucumb. I was lying on my back, unable to move since the day of surgery. They measured my body and I let them do what they wanted. Three days later, Dr. Cucumb entered my bedroom with the orthotist and with Dr. Maker, the orthopedist who had been his partner during the surgery. They were ready to try my new body cast on me.

Without making me sit or stand up, they put this brace around my body. When it was installed and locked, they taught me how to get out of my bed with it around me. Then they helped me stand up and try to walk. Both doctors were holding me when I fainted. That was the end of my lesson for the day.

The next day, Dr. Cucumb and a nurse came back in my bedroom to help me stand up. I had slept all night with the cast on. I did better the second time. I wanted to walk so badly, that I learned how to move with the brace around me. I never took it off except when I was taking my shower. It took six months for me to heal, but I did it.

For three months, a private nurse stayed at my residence. I was allowed to go to the bathroom and take my shower. The nurse would help me out of bed, walk me into the bathroom, help me take my shower, brush my teeth, and put me back to bed. At mealtime, she would put the food on the floor beside my bed; I would turn on my side to eat. I couldn't sit at that time.

Each month following the surgery, my driver took me to see Dr. Cucumb at his office. Arlene would put the seat down in the car, and make me lie down.

On December 28th, when I entered Dr. Cucumb's examination room, the nurse helped me lie down on the table. When he arrived, he checked the movement of my legs, and started talking to me about the surgery. He said it was a very difficult surgery to do and he was proud that I did not become paralyzed. While I was on the exam table, he unzipped his pants and pulled out his penis.

"Open your mouth," he said. "I'll show you something." He started moving his penis in my mouth.

"I can't go to your home anymore to make love to you. It is too dangerous and might defuse your vertebrae," he said.

When he finished, he gave me a tissue, helped me to stand up and said, "Put some lipstick on. The nurse will give you an appointment for next month. If you talk with your psychiatrist, don't talk to him about what I did."

Inside of me, I was sick. I felt used. I wondered what he would do if a nurse came into the room when his penis was out.

"Dr. Cucumb, weren't you afraid that a nurse would come in?"

"Don't worry, I told them that I didn't want to be disturbed."

All this happened thirty days following the back surgery that Dr. Cucumb performed on me. It was eleven months after my accident which Dr. Cucumb referred to as my ***"Head Trauma."***

When I came out of the exam room, the nurse made an appointment for February 27th for me. I went to the waiting room to meet Arlene.

"Are you all right?" she asked, "Are you ready to go?"

"Yes," I answered.

"What did he tell you?"

"He wants to see me next month. Here is the date of my next appointment. I'll tell you more when we are outside," I said.

We left the building and Arlene helped me into the car. She drove me back home while asking a lot of questions. I told her about everything Dr. Cucumb had done to me.

"Odette Marie, this doctor is crazy. He made you have oral sex. You should report him to the medical board, he'll lose his license to practice medicine."

"Arlene, would you please just drive me home? I'll talk to my psychiatrist about what Dr. Cucumb did to me. I've had enough for one day, I just want to go home."

On January 21st, 1984, I saw Dr. Krell, my psychiatrist, again. We discussed what I was reliving during the day and night. Scenes from different scenarios of my childhood, my teenage years, and my adulthood passed through my mind. They were easy to relive for my mind because of the brain damage and the coma period, Dr. Krell explained. He encouraged me to keep remembering as much as I could.

He also told me that for Dr. Cucumb to use his patient sexually was wrong. I had mixed feelings regarding Dr. Cucumb. I depended on him. At that time I only understood that I was alive because Dr. Cucumb was there to save me. I felt great confidence in him. The inner ear surgery was done because Dr. Cucumb was there to refer me to a specialist. I wasn't paralyzed because Dr.

Cucumb performed the laminectomy on my back. I was indebted to him.

My friends and the nurses who were taking care of me could call him day and night. Dr. Cucumb was always there. I believe sincerely that at that time of my life, Dr. Cucumb acted as my security guard. I always thought of what he told me earlier. "I didn't let you die when you were comatose, and I won't let you die now."

At the time, my brain was only able to handle one thing at a time. Dr. Cucumb was there to protect me, and that was confirmed by him. When I missed my husband John, Dr. Cucumb would tell me, "Don't cry, my name is also John. Look at me like I'm John."

On January 23rd, 1984, I was hospitalized in Kyung Ok Hospital. Dr. Cucumb wanted me to have medical tests done on my brain and neck, but the hospital where I was didn't have the equipment for computerized tomography *(CT brain scan).* An ambulance took me to a medical center on Michael Drive where a nurse put me on an exam table and secured my head between two supports. Then a machine took pictures of my brain. After this exam was completed, a doctor injected a bottle of white liquid into my right arm and started a new set of brain pictures at the same time. It wasn't very painful physically, but emotionally, I felt very alone.

The next day, I had a second myelogram for my neck and upper back. They still could not find any medical problem. My right arm was always limp and my upper back was extremely painful. The nurse at the hospital remembered me from the day of my accident in 1982. No one from my family nor my in-laws called. I missed Véronique, my daughter, a lot. She's the only person I have in the United States and I love her with all my heart. I depended on her emotionally.

I went for a second *Cat Scan* on January 25th, 1984. My pain seemed to be increasing. Again, I didn't hear from my family. I felt very sorry for myself. I needed moral support. At times I felt that people only thought of themselves.

Two friends whom I met through Véronique, John and Don, called the next day. They picked up my spirits. I was kept hospitalized for a few days for more tests, but the results shed no light on the reason I felt so much pain. I had pain in the right side of the neck, shoulder, right arm, hand, and three fingers. Dr. Cucumb would say, "Odette Marie, when you have brain damage, it's normal for your body to have so much pain."

On several occasions my driver took me to the emergency room at Los Robles Medical Center to get a pain shot. This occurred often, and Arlene or John were always there for me. After several trips to the emergency room, a nurse recommended that we get a doctor who practiced at that hospital. They did not want to have to keep calling Dr. Cucumb at Kyung Ok Hospital. They referred me to a Dr. Labor Edmunds, a neurologist in Thousand Oaks. Arlene drove me to the emergency room for pain shots for a period of a year and a half. It had become a necessity.

I was still in my brace during that period of time. I had a nurse that would take care of me during the day, and Arlene would call Véronique, only eight years old, every day, and bring her TV dinners. The nurse would stay from eight o'clock in the morning to five o'clock in the evening. Arlene would come to my home at five o'clock to help my daughter and me.

On February 27th, 1984, Arlene drove me to Dr. Cucumb and Dr. Maker's offices for a check on my back. The orthopedist was pleased with my recovery. He took a regular X-ray, and after it was developed, said, "I don't see any problem with the fusion."

"Would you tell me why you make me take an X-ray every time I come to your office?" I asked.

"We just bought a new machine, somebody has to pay for it," he laughed.

"Dr. Maker, please tell me the truth."

"That is the truth," he responded.

Arlene and I then went to Dr. Cucumb's office. Before I went in to see him, Arlene told me she wanted to speak with him. When I told him of my continuing pain, Dr. Cucumb explained that it had only been two months since the surgery.

"Of course, you still have pain," he said. "It'll take time before you stop having pain. We didn't touch the left side of your back. We didn't have time. You were asleep for three hours just to repair the right side. We had to awaken you."

"Why did you have to awaken me?"

"We didn't want you to die," he said. "After the right side is well, we can do the surgery on the left side."

When I asked about the pain in my face, arm, and knee, he said he would refer me to other doctors later on for these problems.

"Let's fix one thing at the time," he said. Then his sexual movements started. He repeated the same oral sex scene that he had performed in December.

"My driver, Arlene, is in the waiting room, and she wants to see you," I said.

"What does she want?" Dr. Cucumb asked.

"She just wants to meet you. She wants to see your face."

"What do you want me to tell her?"

"Whatever you want, but just come with me to the waiting room to see her." He did come to meet Arlene.

When we left his office, I told Arlene that the orthopedist

believed that I was healing well. Dr. Cucumb wants to see me in the office on a monthly basis, and he used me sexually again .

On March 28th, 1984, at ten thirty in the morning, I saw Dr. Maker. At this time he released me from wearing the back brace. At ten forty-five in the morning, I saw Dr. Cucumb, and at one o'clock in the afternoon, Arlene drove me to Grate's office for a follow-up regarding my inner ear surgery. My life had become a series of doctor's appointments.

During this time, not one doctor prescribed physical therapy, nor explained to me how to function with this new fused back after my body was finally free from the cast. I was apprehensive. Should I bend my body if I wanted to pick up something on the floor? Could I stand on my tiptoes if I needed to? Could I continue to move my body like I used to for the thirty-seven years of my first life? Everything was questions without any answers. I had to learn by myself what I could or could not do. I didn't have much knowledge in that field and was not very good at it.

On the way home, I asked Arlene to stop at Coldwell Banker Residential Real Estate, so I could now show my friends my freedom from the brace. I told them, "You can put your hands on me now. I don't have a cast anymore." "Are you going to go back to swimming now that your cast is off?" Roger asked.

"I don't know if I can swim."

"Odette Marie, you used to swim the length of the pool every day. Every morning you were there."

"How many feet was I swimming?"

"You were swimming 8,000 feet every morning."

"Would you write this down on a piece of paper?"

"Sure." He wrote down, *8,000 feet, approximately one and a half miles.* I asked him, "How many feet in a mile?" He told me and wrote on another line, *5,280 ft. per mile.   Odette Marie - one and a half mile swim each day.* "This is what you used to do."

" How do you know this?"

"I used to live in the townhouse beside the pool," he said. "Every morning I would see you in the pool for over an hour."

"I will try to swim to see what I can do," I responded. I thanked Roger for the information and promised that I was going to try again to go to the pool.

Later, my daughter, Véronique, took me to the pool with a neighbor she said I used to swim with. I didn't remember it. The lady said, "Odette Marie, if you feel like it, we can go swimming at four thirty or five o'clock in the afternoon. Not many people will be there. I'll come back to get you."

At five o'clock she arrived. She started to show me how to swim. I tried it many times without any success. I had lost the coordination of my movements. With my head in the water, I felt too dizzy, like my head was full of water. My right arm didn't want to function. I had too much pain. It was impossible to move my right leg. My knee and my toes were in pain. Nothing wanted to collaborate. Every movement had been erased by the brain injury, like Dr. Cucumb told me.

I decided to get out of that pool after an hour. The neighbor helped me, and we went back home. She carried my towel and cream. On the left side of my mind, I couldn't accept the loss of not being able to swim. I was disappointed. I had just proved to myself once more what a vegetable I was. I couldn't believe it.

I told myself, this isn't me. I can't believe that the coordination of my body was lost due to my brain injury. I didn't believe it. I didn't believe Dr. Cucumb.

Why did I have such pain? If it was only my brain that was

creating these problems, I wouldn't have aches all over my body. I decided I was going to prove that the brain injury was one thing, and the balance of my body movements another.

Meanwhile, I knew that exercise would be good for me. The next day I started walking. Véronique came along, and we walked around the block one time. After that day we walked every morning. I had pain in my back, legs, foot and right toes, but I couldn't stop. I forced myself to tolerate the pain. Afterall, Dr. Cucumb said that these problems were in my brain, no place else.

CHAPTER 11
MORE DOCTORS AND DENTISTS

In June of 1984, I told Arlene I wanted to drive myself to the drug store on Borchard Road in Newbury Park. It was only five minutes from my home and I needed to pick up a prescription. She agreed, and told me to call her at her office if I needed her. After I picked up my medicine and was leaving the parking lot, the traffic signal turned green and I proceeded into the intersection slowly. Suddenly, a big truck came down Borchard road, and ran the red light, destroying the side of my car. I knew my back had been injured again. Traffic was completely blocked by the accident, and screaming sirens signaled the arrival of the police.

The driver of the truck approached my car, opened the door and spoke to me.

"Can you get out of the car?"

"I have a lot of back pain, and I can't get out of here," I cried. He apologized and asked for my name, which I gave him. "Are you John Kuhlman's wife?" His eyes were wide.

"Yes, I am."

"I'm so sorry for this accident. I knew your husband. We used to work for the same company."

By this time an ambulance had arrived, and with the help of the attendants, they took me to Los Robles Medical Center. I was experiencing severe back pain.

The doctor in the emergency room wanted to keep me overnight at the hospital, but I refused. I explained, "My daughter is only nine years old and she was asleep at home when I left. I need to be with her when she wakes up."

"Can you call your husband?"

"We had an accident not long ago, my husband is dead. My daughter has only me, I must go home."

"Could you call a neighbor? You aren't going to be able to do anything by leaving the hospital."

I called Arlene and told her that I had just re-injured my back, and I was in the hospital. I asked her if she could talk to my neighbor, and go to my home to check Véronique. Arlene did just that. She took care of Véronique and told her that she was coming to pick me up at the hospital. She cautioned her not to worry. When we arrived home, my neighbor, Colleen, was with my daughter.

After this accident I had so much back and neck pain, I could hardly function. On June 27th, 1984, Dr. Cucumb arranged for me to take a **Cat Scan** at Los Robles Medical Center for neck pain. I had myo-facial pain and headaches that didn't make sense. Why couldn't Dr. Cucumb or other doctors find a reason for my pain and offer me some relief? That was my question. I had lots of prescriptions for pain pills, but they didn't help. Every morning I woke up to physical pain.

I asked Dr. Cucumb, "You're the doctor, you should know what creates the pain." The answer was always, "It's your brain injury that creates the pain. Also, your car accident didn't help. You don't need any more accidents of any kind."

"What about the pain in my right arm, my hand, and fingers. And, how come I can't drive? I can't use my right foot for the gasoline pedal or to brake. Is it also my brain damage that causes that pain?"

"Odette Marie, the entire right side of your body is affected by the brain trauma that you suffered, and five days ago, you had another accident. That also doesn't help your back."

So, I continued to take pain pills by the dozen, day and night. According to Dr. Cucumb there was no other solution to rescue me from this physical pain.

For one year and nine months during the rehabilitation process, I was alone with Véronique. I wanted so much to understand what was happening to my brain, so I decided to go to Moorpark College and study psychology. I was determined to find an answer. I reserved a spot in a psychology class in the summer of 1984. With Arlene's help, I attended class every day even though it was a struggle.

After the automobile accident, on June 28th, 1984, I experienced so much pain in my back and right leg, that a student from our class had to drive me home. I couldn't stay any longer. Once again physical pain was barring me from achieving my goals. The Newbury Park automobile accident aggravated my problems.

I felt more helpless, questioning God again. What did he want from me? I was doing everything I could to advance in life, and something always happened. I was ambitious and persevering. I read my psychology book and did all the chapter tests during the time I was confined to bed due to pain. I kept telling myself nothing would stop me from relearning, even if I couldn't walk or drive to attend college.

On July 3rd, 1984, I had a psychotherapy session with Dr.

Krell. I was seeing him three times a week. I told him about the automobile accident and my frustration with pain.

"Odette Marie, you have to write a book. People live up to eighty years of age and don't have one quarter of the action in their life like you have in yours. There is so much in your life, you should let people know. I told you this after your first accident. Write a book!"

After that session with Dr. Krell, I decided to write this book. I felt he was right. Perhaps I could help others by telling my story.

During my visit in July to Dr. Cucumb, he suggested that I move to a one story home. It would help my condition not to have to go up and down the stairs to go to the bedroom and bathroom. Because I was dizzy all the time, he didn't want me to fall down the stairs and hurt myself. When I came out of his office, Arlene was in the waiting room.

"What did he say, Odette Marie? What is he going to do for the pain that you have?"

"He wants me to move to a one story home and he gave me one more prescription," I said. "Dr. Cucumb is well situated to advise me regarding the home I should have. He comes to my house so often, he knows what I need."

We left Dr. Cucumb's office and Arlene drove me to Dr. Maker and Dr. Grate's offices. I mentioned Dr. Cucumb's advice to them and they agreed.

Arlene, being a real estate agent, started to look on the real estate market to find me a home. She knew exactly what I needed and visited many properties for me. I was unable to go with her to preview homes and told her, "When you find what I need, let me know and I'll make an offer."

Later she came to see me and said, "Odette Marie, I found

exactly what you need. It's a townhouse, with a huge garage with a garage door opener. It's all fenced, and from the backyard there is a beautiful view."

"Where is this place? How many bedrooms? I need a room for my office."

"Come with me to see it. It's in the Racquet Club Villas. An older couple owns this townhouse and they have a little dog. They keep their home very beautifully," she said.

Véronique, Arlene and I went to see the property. Arlene was right. The floor plan was perfect for my needs and Véronique fell in love with the miniature schnauzer named *Fritz.* We returned home and I talked with my lawyer, Mr. Koosch, about the new property. Arlene and I met with him on August 17th and she presented the paperwork. After looking it over, he agreed to the purchase. We both signed the offer. The next day Arlene presented the purchase agreement to the seller. It was accepted and escrow closed on September 25th, 1984. Ah! I forgot to tell you that the dog, *Fritz,* came with the property. Véronique was overjoyed. For my daughter and me, it was one more move ahead in my recovery.

When someone you love, like your husband or father, dies, even if they are no longer with you, they live on in your memory. Sometimes you can see them opening the front door, sitting on the sofa, relaxing around the table. I often felt John coming close to my bed to kiss me. Véronique felt his presence too. That was what we were feeling.

"It doesn't matter if daddy is dead, mother, I can see him, and feel him. He knows where I put my bike in the garage."

"Yes, honey. I understand."

"Mom, if we buy a new home, it will be a new beginning for you and me."

She was absolutely right.

In January, 1985, I again visited Dr. Cucumb's office with so much facial and neck pain, I felt I was going crazy. He told me that he could take care of my back, but that the brain injury was creating the pain in my neck and there was nothing he could do about it. Only time was going to cure the medical problem. My brain needed to stabilize.

I could no longer live with the pain. I went over in my mind all the different doctors I had seen since I came out of the coma. The only one missing that I could think of was a dentist. So, I called a friend, Hillary, to find out if her boss, a children's dentist, could refer me to someone. The next day she gave me the name of an orthodontist in Oxnard, Dr. Weber.

The first thing I did the following morning was to call Dr. Weber for an appointment. I was able to see him January 18th, and explained the pain on one side of my face. My teeth were sore, my cheek, nose, eyes and forehead ached. I told him about the accident, how I was comatose, and that I had brain damage. I explained how Dr. Cucumb thought the brain was creating my pain.

"Let me take some X-rays of your teeth and I'll tell you what I can do," Dr. Weber said.

He took X-rays of my mouth and told me that the clicking noise I heard in my jaw was caused by a broken bone, but because of the years that has passed, the broken bone fused itself in a bad position. The upper teeth weren't meeting with the lower teeth. In addition, he said I had tensing facial muscles.

"What do you mean my teeth aren't coming together?"

He explained that when teeth come together, every tooth is supposed to have a perfect bite. In my case, my bite was misaligned.

"How can I put my teeth back where they belong?"

"To align them, I will have to cover your teeth with crowns. I have a patient right now who also suffers from myo-facial pain disfunction like you. I installed crowns on the upper and lower teeth on her and it took care of all facial and tooth pain."

"How do you install crowns?" I asked.

"The teeth must be ground down to make room for the crowns," he answered.

"Would I lose my teeth?"

"No, your teeth will be under the crowns."

"How much will it cost me?" I asked.

"Between 10,000 and 15,000 dollars." He asked about my insurance.

"Yes, I have health insurance. But, you have to have authorization from the insurance company first to see if they'll cover the bill. Otherwise, they will refuse to pay."

I told Dr. Weber that I wanted to get another opinion. I did not want to lose my teeth, and felt that if crowns were put on, I would lose my natural teeth.

"Fine, Mrs. Kuhlman. Let me give you an appointment for January 25th at nine o'clock for the tensing facial muscles," he said.

I went to see the dentist that took care of my teeth before my accident. After I explained my situation, he said that the best course of action would be to remove all my teeth and wear dentures. In his opinion, installing crowns was his second option because the price to get this done was exorbitant compared to dentures. For a few hundred dollars, I could have dentures instead of paying 15,000 dollars for crowns.

Discouraged, I told him, "Thank you, doctor, for your opinion, but I'm not going to lose one tooth. No matter what."

I left his office, and I never went back.

I explained to my neurologist what the dentists had told me and he said, "Odette Marie, you should get your teeth fixed. It's probably the only treatment."

I was stubborn. "Doctor, for sure I won't let anyone touch my teeth. It doesn't matter what these dentists say. No one will remove any of my teeth." I was getting more angry every day.

When I visited Dr. Weber's office concerning therapy for my tensing facial muscles, the first thing the doctor did when I arrived was to introduce me to the female patient who had crowns installed everywhere in her mouth. She told me how fantastic it was; no more facial pain, no worry about her teeth anymore, etc. I listened to what she had to say. Then the nurse asked me to go with her while she taught me the therapy for my jaw and facial muscles. It took over two hours. In addition, Dr. Weber gave me a prescription for more pain pills.

That afternoon, I kept another appointment with a different dentist in Oxnard. He also informed me that even though my teeth were healthy and beautiful, the only way to eliminate the pain was to get them removed and wear dentures. I thanked him for his opinion and left his office. I never went back.

For the time being, the only solution that I had was to continue the physical therapy for my tensing facial muscle. It did help my muscles, but I still experienced pain in my face and head.

Dr. Weber said, "We did try to free you from that physical pain without putting crowns on your teeth, but it appears that the only solution, Odette Marie, is to let me put crowns on your teeth."

I explained that I was going in for a second surgery on my back in February, and after this was done, I would consider what he told me.

My mind began questioning the competence of the doctors and dentists I had visited. I was desperate to get rid of my facial pain. I was very stubborn; I knew the pain I had was physical, and I was determined to find a competent orthodontist that would fix the jaw problem *(Temporomandibular Joint - TMJ)* I was suffering from.

I visited eight dentists in Oxnard, Alhambra, El Monte, Pasadena, Los Angeles, Thousand Oaks, and Westlake Village. Three of them had similar answers, "We don't know exactly what creates the pain. You have beautiful teeth. But, maybe by putting crowns on your teeth, it might remove the pain. We'll only know the answer after it has been done. After a brain injury, it's normal that you have facial pain."

After looking at my X-rays, one told me that he needed a different type of exam before he could tell me what was wrong. At my next appointment, this dentist entered the exam room and informed me that I had two choices, "Get all your teeth removed and wear dentures, or get crowns on every tooth." He continued telling me, "This will remove the facial pain, jaw and tooth pain. It'll cost a few hundred dollars to get your teeth removed if you choose that option. If you choose the second option, it'll cost approximately 15,000 dollars."

I stared at the orthodontist and told him, "I lost my health in this accident, I lost my husband in this accident, but I'll not lose one of my natural teeth. I'm going to see every orthodontist in Los Angeles if I have to, but I'll save my teeth."

CHAPTER 12 - SELF ESTEEM AND SECURITY

The time had arrived for picking up the pieces regarding my professional life in real estate. If I was to keep my license, I had to renew it in 1984. Arlene and I took the necessary courses together to earn our forty-five hours and obtain our license renewal for another four years. We went to Simi Valley Board of Realtors, Conejo Valley Board of Realtors, Coldwell Banker Residential Real Estate, and to Moorpark College.

I was unable to sit because of back pain so I stood up for a while and laid on the floor for the balance of the course. I would always use the last row in the classroom, so as not to disturb the other students. Arlene would help me to lie down when it was necessary or stand up. She never left me alone and came everywhere with me for support. In addition, she took good care of the clients that I had in real estate before I was injured. She had the capacity to make everyone happy by her professionalism. Without Arlene, I wouldn't have been able to renew my real estate license. She was such a big help, like an angel to me; there to teach me what I needed to know and keep me on track.

I worked very hard to renew and keep my license. Even today, I can say I lost a lot in the mountain accident, but I never did lose my real estate license! Every four years, I renewed it. It was, and still is, important to me.

After I married John, for a long time I considered becoming an American citizen like my husband. We discussed it and John agreed with me. Having a green card was fine for a while, but the moment I became eligible under immigration law, becoming an American was of primary importance.

In October of 1982, I applied for my new citizenship and John also applied for our daughter, Véronique. John was born an American and I felt that it would be nice if Véronique, Korean born and French Canadian adopted, could also become an American. It was important in my life to be an American like John. No more Canadian, Korean, and American family. Both John and I felt that to have our family be the same nationality was a good idea.

I remembered one time I told John, "Sweetheart, if something happened to you, I wouldn't feel secure with only a green card. This wouldn't be my country. If I become an American, this will be my country. To me, this is security."

John signed the citizenship forms for our daughter in October, 1982. The following December, he died in the mountain accident. When the lady from immigration contacted us for the test, I told her that John was dead. My lawyer could explain our situation. She agreed to speak with my lawyer and set up an appointment for us. I took time to talk with Véronique about it, and we both decided that this was the last gift that John, my husband and her father, was giving us; a new citizenship. In honor of John, on May 13th, 1984, we became American citizens.

These phases of my life helped me to survive. Just being alive, being a mother, stubborn enough to renew my real estate license, and becoming an American; I finally had something to live for. Being a mother is the greatest position that exists, but I also needed something to make me feel more secure.

In September of 1984 Arlene drove me to my psychologist, Dr. Ettinger, in Westlake Village. He was the fifth one that I had seen. Still unsettled, I would change doctors every so many months, searching for one that could tell me that John was not dead, that this accident had not happened, that I would be able to remember. I was still in denial and longed to be myself again, capable like I used to be.

Between 1983 and 1985, I visited nine psychiatrists or psychologists. It was a terrible time. I was in denial, hardly capable of coping with life, dealing with great pain and always believing that John would come back. I was lonely and afraid.

During one session, Dr. Ettinger told me that it might be a good idea to visit Parents Without Partners, (P.W.P.). He explained to me that this was an association of divorced parents, and widows and widowers who have children and wanted to meet new friends. He said it was important for my child and I to go there. "You need to rebuild your life," he said.

"But I don't want to meet a divorced man. I don't need more problems, I have enough of my own."

"Go there. You might meet a widower. You won't know until you try."

Dr. Ettinger gave Arlene the address and telephone number of P.W.P. He told her, "Be sure that you drive Odette Marie there, and I recommend that you stay with her."

On Friday, the 14th of September, Arlene and I went to P.W.P. in Thousand Oaks after arranging for a babysitter for Véronique. We both became members of the association during the meeting.

When the speaker asked if there were new members present, we put our hands up. He asked us if we were divorced or widowed. Besides us, one new member, a handsome widower, and I were the only ones widowed. This one might be for me, I thought.

On September 21st, we attended a P.W.P. party at the home of the president. We met all the new members more intimately, and naturally, the tall elegant widower was there. Having a lot in common, we spent most of the evening together talking. I asked him how he had become a widower so young. He asked how my husband had died. We both asked about children.

At the end of the evening, he asked to drive me home. I explained about my driver.

"Let me speak with your driver," he said. He met Arlene and told her that he wanted to drive me home.

"I'm going to drive Odette Marie home tonight because I'm responsible for her," Arlene said. "I have to take care of her, but if Odette Marie wants, I can give you her phone number and address. You can call later and visit her, but not tonight."

So I gave my notebook (*agenda*) to the widower and asked if he could write his name on the day's page. Smiling, he wrote, "David Fischer," his telephone number, and a short sentence, "I play racquetball, would you like to learn to play?"

The day after, he called me and came to my home. Because I was unable to sit or stand up for long periods, I had to receive him in my bedroom. David met my daughter and we played backgammon on the bed all evening. From then on, he would call in the afternoon and invite Véronique and me for dinner. We met his son, Ed, who was sixteen years old. My daughter and I liked him very much.

David had many friends. For almost a year, every week we were invited for dinner at someone's home. I learned that David was Jewish, a new discovery for me. I had never gone out with a Jewish man or eaten Jewish food before. All my boyfriends since I was fifteen years of age, including my deceased husband, were Catholic.

Jewish men have a special way of thinking and acting towards a lady. It was so different. David made me feel secure and wanted. To him, I was a Jewish princess. My handicap didn't stop him from loving me. Although my brain wasn't stable at the time, and I often repeated myself over and over on the subject of the accident and what my family had done following John's death, David and his friends were always there to listen.

It didn't matter if they were listening to be polite, or just to make me feel happy. Ninety-seven percent of David's friends had the capacity to see how injured I was, and were able to accept me just the way I was. At that time, I was confused and frightened. David provided physical reassurance. He had a calm voice and helped me in my recovery. He would let me depend on him emotionally and physically. In addition, when available, he would drive me to my doctors and meet them. His arrival into our lives was a complete new phase for Véronique's and my future.

I proudly told Dr. Krell, my psychiatrist, about meeting my Jewish widower, a beautiful person. I did realize that David coming into my life was not going to cure all the intellectual, emotional and physical pain, but just his being there every night for sharing and caring met my needs. He was good for my soul.

I was able to tell him of the sexual harassments of Dr. Cucumb. I felt emotionally secure with David. It was easy for me to share my feelings with him. We both needed love and understanding.

David wanted to introduce me to a psychologist in Westlake

Village.

"I know him. When my wife was sick, and after she died, I went to see Dr. Tyra. He's very good, he'll help you, and you can talk to him about everything, especially about your neurosurgeon's sexual advances," he said. "Should this doctor continue to be your physician, Odette Marie? You can ask Dr. Tyra about it."

I saw the new psychologist in September of 1984. David came with me for the first session. After Dr. Tyra learned from David about my injuries, the following sessions I saw him alone. I thought he was a nice person, but professionally, I wasn't pleased with him. He always wanted me to cry. He couldn't understand that I was unable to do it. I was so wrapped in anger and pain, I just couldn't cry. I didn't know how to do it. Even though crying might have helped me, my eyes could not release any tears. I was lost.

Dr. Tyra would ask me, "Do you know where the accident happened?"

"I don't know. I don't have any idea where it is. My lawyer gave me the name of the canyon where it happened, but I don't remember," I replied.

"Next time I see you, bring me the name of that canyon. I'll tell you where it is. It' ll help you to remember."

I discussed with him, like I did with the other psychiatrists and psychologists, the secret that Dr. Cucumb wanted me to keep about his sexual advances. This doctor was like all the other ones, trying to convince me to say no to the surgeon regarding his sexual needs.

"Odette Marie, you have a boyfriend now," Dr. Tyra said. "David is there with you, and he's a very good man. You must keep in mind that you must say no to this surgeon. He would lose his license to practice medicine if you report him. What he is doing isn't normal. This doctor is using you."

Inside, I began to feel that what Dr. Cucumb was doing to me was wrong. But, he was my security regarding my back. He had promised he would never let me become paralyzed. That was so important to me, to be able to walk and raise my daughter. I had already lost enough. I didn't want to lose the capacity of being able to walk.

David told me over and over, "I'll find you an excellent neurosurgeon in the Los Angeles area. One that will not use you. Dr. Cucumb is using you. I'm going to call Ron and Mike (relatives of his). They are doctors themselves. I'll ask them to refer you to someone very competent."

In November, I told Dr. Tyra that I was going to see Dr. Cucumb at his office for a follow-up. He prepared me to handle Dr. Cucumb in a polite way. At that phase of my life, I was so afraid to hurt someone. I felt that I had poor contact with people and, being my primary physician, Dr. Cucumb played a huge role in my recovery. He always told me he did.

Arlene took me to Dr. Cucumb's office and said, "Odette Marie, don't let Dr. Cucumb caress you. If he takes his penis out of his pants, scream. Tell him you'll report him to the Medical Board. I'll be waiting for you here. If you need me, I'll help you."

I'll never forget that appointment. While Dr. Cucumb examined my back and legs, I told him I had a boyfriend and that he was in the waiting room.

"Would you like to meet him?" I asked.

His face fell in distress. "You can go now. I'll see you next month," he said. He wouldn't meet my eyes. I could feel his distance. He became angry.

Inside, I felt I had no choice, but lie to my physician *by telling him that David was in the waiting room.* I had to tell Dr. Cucumb something while he was examining me. I wasn't at ease with him. I was afraid to hurt him and scared that he wouldn't treat me as a patient anymore. For so long, psychiatrists and psychologists had told me to tell Dr. Cucumb not to sexually touch me. Before that day, I was totally unable to do this.

On November 27th, I met with Dr. Tyra again and told him of my meeting with Dr. Cucumb. I also showed him a paper with the name of the mountain where John, and I had the accident. He knew where it was and asked me to go there with him. I could not go there. I was too afraid. He gave me his personal address and telephone number.

"Odette Marie, if you decide to go see the mountain, give me a call. I live in the Racquet Club Villas too, very close to where you live."

Throughout this time, I continued to have neck, face and back pain. On many occasions David drove me to emergency clinics for injections. In spite of many more tests, the doctors were unable to find reasons. This period of calling orthopedist doctors and neurosurgeons for pain shots and prescriptions continued until February 3rd, 1985. But renewing my real estate license and meeting David had brought some comfort to my life. My needs were being met. I was slowly learning to stand up for myself and exert some control over my medical condition.

CHAPTER 13 - FORGOTTEN FRIENDS
BRAIN CELLS

During this time I heard from many people I had known in my past life. While I could remember some of their names, most often I could not recall their faces or anything else. Names held a vague familiarity, that was all I could comprehend.

In July of 1983, I received a telephone call from Marcello Danon, the executive producer of "La Cage Aux Folles" motion picture. He invited me for dinner. I told Marcello that I didn't remember his face, but I did recall his name and the title of the motion picture.

"How come you don't remember me, Odette Marie? We've known each other for over a year." I explained the accident, how I had been comatose, and my subsequent lack of memory. I declined an invitation to meet with him.

"Where did I meet you?" I asked.

"We met at Columbia Pictures in 1981," he said. He asked me questions about the accident, and then told me that he and his daughter were going to be in Beverly Hills for the entire summer. I received more phone calls from Marcello, but I was unable to accept any invitations from him because of my illness.

"When I feel better, I will come to see you in Rome. Maybe you can make a movie about my accident," I laughed. We then talked a little bit more about scripts, filming and the importance of copyright. It was frustrating to be so confused and remember so little of my first life.

In August of 1983, I had great pain in my right leg and foot which caused difficulty walking. Headaches plagued my every day and night. I always felt dizzy.

I still felt tremendous anger about the accident. Why had God let this happen. The psychiatrists, Dr. Andreassen, as well as Dr. Krell, would tell me on every visit, "Odette Marie, God didn't punish you. You had an accident. It can happen to anyone. What members of your family did was wrong. Do not worry about your sisters and your brother, they live in another country. Your brother-in-law reported them to the police. They won't come to Los Angeles to kidnap your daughter anymore."

They continued to tell me that what Dr. Cucumb was doing to me sexually was wrong, and unprofessional. They told me he should be reported to the Medical Board of California, and I should refuse to see him anymore.

They explained that the brain injury created a lot of problems in my body. This was the reason for my pain and for my lack of memory and ability to perform simple tasks like cooking. According to them, it would take five years before my brain would stabilize. Some day, they said, you'll be able to be back on the air, have a professional life again. It'll take time, but, you can do it.

I struggled to believe them. My life seemed so hopeless and full of pain. I was raised in the Catholic religion, and as a child had been taught that God is all powerful. He knows what is going to happen to us before it happens. But isn't he also suppose to protect us? Why didn't he protect me?

On the 19th of September, 1983, at one o'clock in the morning, I became so depressed that I thought Véronique and I might as well be dead, to be with John. I could only remember the good times when we were married. I wanted that back again.

In a panic, I called Dr. Krell to tell him how I felt, that I was thinking of suicide, that I felt like a prostitute because of what Dr. Cucumb was doing to me. I desperately needed to feel loved. I was very unstable.

"Ask your lady driver to stay with you until you fall asleep," Dr. Krell said. "Your feelings are normal with a damaged brain like you have. When your brain has stabilized, these feelings will go away. Don't worry. I just want you to call your driver now. I don't want you to be alone. Tell your driver to call me."

Seeing a psychiatrist regularly helped me to face the facts of my loss, and learn how to cope and accept my brain trauma. My mood levels would fluctuate because I had lost track of my life. It was a very difficult period.

I saw up to seven psychiatrists/psychologists, one after the other, for a long period of time, hoping that one of them could repair my brain. I had headaches all day and woke up every night to take aspirin with codeine. I also had tremendous pain in my right leg and foot and couldn't concentrate. I felt unbalanced. My eyes gave me problems and my sight was tangled even at short distances.

One neuropsychiarist told me, "Why don't you watch some television programs and try to remember what you see and hear? That should help stabilize your brain and you might regain some of your lost memory." I was willing to do anything to get my brain back on track, to regain normal memory.

After visiting the doctor, Véronique asked me, "What did the doctor say, Mom?"I explained how he had recommended that I try watching television programs.

"Mom, I know which channels you like the most. Let me put the television on the channel that you used to look at before the accident." She took the remote control and selected channel 7.

"You always enjoyed looking at this TV channel. Maybe you'll remember."

We watched channel 7, but I couldn't remember any faces, nor any names. Véronique played with the remote control for a long time. She tried every channel, but nothing registered in my brain. I needed an entire relearning process.

Finally at 6:00 p.m. the same day, Véronique said, "Mom, this is the time that you used to look at the news. Let's put it back on channel 7."

I looked at the faces of the news anchors but, I couldn't remember their names, with the exception of one lady. "This lady with white hair, I have seen her before," I said to Véronique. "I think her name is . . . Christine. Listen to what they say and tell me if the name I said is correct, because I'm not sure." Véronique listened very closely.

Later during the news cast, I told my daughter, "That is Dr. George. I know him. He used to do the weather broadcast." I was very excited. "I remember him. I know him." We embraced each other, very happy with my memory. Dr. George on channel 7 was the only man that I was able to recall, and I remembered his name and his personality. He was the only TV personality that wasn't a stranger to me. Remembering him so well made me feel secure, and gave me hope that I might retrieve more from my damaged brain.

Thanks to Dr. George and Christine Lund of channel 7, I felt there was a chance I could recover, and not remain a vegetable. I began to watch television every day. Even if I was unable to catch what they were saying, my first step was to relearn their names, and try not to forget what they looked like.

In December of 1984 I received a telephone call from a Dr. Omar Lahlou in Florida, who asked if Véronique and I would like to spend Christmas vacation with him at his hotel.

"How did you find my telephone number? Who told you that I was a widow?"

"Odette Marie, before I left Lévis to go to Florida, I called your mother. She told me of the accident, and about John's death. I asked her for your telephone number. I wanted to speak with you."

"I remember your name. But, I can't recall your face. I don't know what you look like, nor where I met you," I said.

"Don't you remember I bought your companies in 1975?" he said.

"Other friends from Québec have called to find out how I am too," I said. "They heard about the accident in the news, and I can't recall these people either. They told me that I was president of two companies. I didn't have any idea what they were talking about."

"Do you remember the computer science college you founded in 1968?" he asked.

"I have the paperwork here that tells me I was the director of a college. A friend of mine from Québec came to Los Angeles and showed me all the files in my office. I saw permits from the government of Québec which show that I was director of *Institut Professionnel d'Informatique, Inc.,* but, that doesn't tell me who you are."

Dr. Lahlou said, "In 1975, I met you at your office following publicity you had run in the newspapers for the sale of the college.

And, because it was in the field that I specialized in, I decided to invest in your company."

"What are you doing in Florida? What about the college?" I asked.

"Now, I've invested in a hotel, this is why I'm here. I bought a hotel in Daytona Beach, and I'm here for the holiday season. Don't you remember, Odette Marie, that we filed bankruptcy for I.P.I. Inc., because the Ministere of Education refused to give me a permit to operate the college as director after I bought it?"

"No, I don't know what you're talking about. But, tell me about it," I said.

"I'm busy now but I'll call you tomorrow and explain everything," he said.

Dr. Lahlou called back the next evening. I was excited. This was going to be a chance to relearn about another phase of my first life.

He told me, "In private education, the permit to operate a private college has to be renewed in June of each year. In April, 1976, I prepared the educational program that I wanted to teach, beginning in July, 1976. I applied to the Ministere of Education for approval, and to renew the permit. In May, 1977, I received a letter addressed to your name, and to our company's name. It was from the General Director of the private education service and informed us that the permit could not be renewed due to insufficiency at the general administration level. Because I work full time at College d'Enseignement General et Professionnel (C.E.G.E.P.) at Lévis-Lauzon, the General Director said that I could not be director of a private college at the same time."

"Did you close the college because of that?" I asked.

"Not really, it was the first time the foundation of the *Institut*

Professionnel d'Informatique, Inc., since it was created in 1968, that denial of permission to operate was issued by the Ministere of Education."

"What did you do?" I asked.

"Don't you remember? I called you immediately after I received the letter. We discussed it, and you flew to Québec to take care of this problem," Dr. Lahlou said.

I listened to what he was telling me, but did not know what to think.

"We had many meetings with the General Director of the government, and the answer was that because you were living in California and didn't have any more responsibility toward the students of the college, and I was working full time at the public college, the permit couldn't be given. My only way to keep the college open would have been to engage more people to work at the general administration level, and I wasn't in a financial position to do that."

Dr. Lahlou and I talked together for over an hour that evening on the subject of I.P.I., Inc. Two days later, my friend, Arlene, was at my home when Dr. Lahlou called me for the third time. He told me about the final disposition of *Institut Professionnel d'Informatique, Inc.*

Apparently, at our last meeting with the General Director of the private education department, I asked what was needed in order to keep the college open. We had students to take care of, their courses weren't completed, and we couldn't just close the college. The answer from the General Director was simple for him, but terrible for us. He told us we must close the college. All of the students would be transferred to public college, and could complete their courses there. They wouldn't lose anything.

Dr. Lahlou went on, "We told the director that I.P.I. had

monthly payments to make on the equipment. We didn't operate a business for nine years to just close it like that."

"Don't register any more students," the General Director said. "Let the bills of the business pile up. Pay salaries and rent with the money that I.P.I. has. Later on, when you have enough bills, go to the syndics of Caliza Lavalée, see Mr. Moyelle, and tell him that you want to sign the necessary papers to put the company into bankruptcy. Don't worry about anything. Mr. Moyelle will take care of the company, and we'll take care of the students," the General Director told us.

"That was a nightmare," Dr. Lahlou said. "You and I had no knowledge about bankruptcy. We never thought of bankrupting the company. After the meeting with the General Director, we spent a few weeks trying to find a solution. I felt that I could handle both positions. But, the private education service's director couldn't understand my capacity. Your new residence was with John and your daughter in California. Therefore, we had no recourse, except to do exactly what we were advised to do. We both went to see Mr. Moyelle at the syndics and explained the situation.

Dr. Lahlou told me that the syndics man was very understanding. He advised us not to open the college the next day because he was going to install a sign at the front door instructing the students to contact with him. He would take care of the bills that had accumulated.

Following our conversation, I felt that I had closed another door of my career. It made me realize that often in life, we close one door to open a new one. All we can do is our best in every scenario that is created.

During my last conversation with Dr. Lahlou, to my surprise, he asked me to marry him. He invited my daughter and I to go to

Daytona Beach, Florida, but the situation was impossible because of my physical condition.

He then decided that after the holiday season, he was going to come to Los Angeles to talk more about our marriage. At the same time he was going to research investment in more hotels. I told him that he was welcome to come to Los Angeles to my residence, but I wasn't going to marry him or anyone else. I was not ready to get remarried.

Following that, he spoke with my girlfriend, Arlene, about real estate. She was going to do a preview of a hotel in the Conejo Valley to show him during his trip to Los Angeles. The entire conversation had my mind reeling, trying to recall these past events. A week later, Dr. Lahlou called to find out how I was feeling. He said he was anxious to see Véronique and I.

In January he called to postpone his trip to Los Angeles because he had a problem with his legs. In the middle of the month, I received a telephone call from mother giving me the sad news. Dr. Omar Lahlou had died in Florida on January 16th.

"He was supposed to be here at the end of the month. He wanted me to marry him, and he was going to invest in Los Angeles. How did you find out he died, mother?"

"It was on the radio and in the newspaper," she said.

I felt terrible when mother told me of Dr. Lahlou's death. She said, "Odette Marie, if you had married Omar, you would have been a widow again." I contacted members of his family to offer them my condolence.

This was one more scenario of my life that was closed forever. But, I had the chance to relearn from Dr. Lahlou, and that was a precious segment. I would have liked to have talked more with him, to have seen him. But, our destiny was not lined up that way.

Each of us has a destiny, no matter which country we are in. When we're born, there is a road already designed for us. We grow up not knowing about it, but destiny keeps us on the road that God planned.

Another old friend, my co-producer, Maria-Estela Lorca, from Buenos Aires, Argentina, would call every two weeks. I explained to her that I knew her name but could not remember anything more. I asked if she could come to Hollywood and visit me at the same time.

"Julio and I are going to Cuba. We are invited by Fidel Castro. I'll ask Julio if we could also go to Hollywood before coming back to Buenos Aires. I'll call you back before we leave to let you know."

The more she called, the more I wanted to remember her. It became very important to me to recall who she was, what she looked like and what we used to produce together. When she called, she would always ask, "When can you come back to work? There are so many things that we have to produce, and Odette Marie, I enjoyed producing with you." The only thing that I could say to Maria-Estela was, "You can't believe how injured I am. I don't have any idea if I'll ever be able to produce again. When you come to visit me, you'll realize that I'm not the same Odette Marie Kuhlman that you knew."

Maria-Estela called and said that she and Julio would be in California on January 7th. She asked if I could pick them up at Los Angeles International Airport.

"I'll be at the airport at the luggage department," I said. "I don't know if I'll recognize you, but I'll be there for sure." She gave me her flight number, time of arrival and told me what she would be wearing. Véronique was very excited to find out that Maria-Estela and Julio De Grazia were coming to visit us. She wanted to come with me to the airport to pick them up.

"Mom, I know Maria-Estela well, she used to sleep at our home before the accident. I'll know who she is, can I go with you to the airport? You'll see Mom, I'll help you." One more time, I was going to depend on my daughter.

We both went to the airport and I realized I would never have remembered my friends. This part of my memory had been erased. Maria-Estela recognized me, and Véronique knew who she was immediately. Very excited, she told me, "Mom, this is Maria-Estela. Don't you remember her? You used to work together."

We had the pleasure of being together for one week. During this time, Maria-Estela suggested that I go with her to buy a VCR. She wanted to teach me how to use one like I used to. But after a week of trying, learning to operate the machine escaped me. When Maria-Estela and Julio left my home to go back to Argentina, I was still unable to operate the VCR.

After their departure for Buenos Aires, other friends tried to teach me how to use the VCR, but it took one year of instruction and practice before I was able to operate the machine completely alone. With the help of my friends, I relearned. I felt that I had taken a step in the right direction. I had bought an important tool to work with toward my recovery.

I was so discouraged when I would hear what people told me about my forgotten first life. I needed to confirm what people were telling me. I would make telephone calls to Québec and speak with friends to verify what my brain was retrieving. I felt that nothing was balanced any longer. My head was full of water since waking from the coma due to swelling of the brain caused by the accident.

I was living on hope. I wanted to go back to work as a talent

(TV host) and producer, plus maintain my real estate license, to be independent and successful like I had always been, according to my friends.

In November of 1988, I started to retrieve more information. I could see the color of a dress this lady was wearing when she got married. I was able to remember her name and where she used to work. But, I couldn't picture her face. I just felt close to her. I knew that I liked and respected her. But, who was she? What did she look like? (I had really had enough of this lost memory coming back.) I had to see if this person existed.

I knew her employer's name, so I called the operator in Québec City, and asked for the telephone number of St. François d'Assise hospital. After I got the information, I called and asked to speak with Sarah Bouline. The receptionist informed me that there were two Sarah Boulines who worked there. Which one did I want to speak with. I didn't know the answer. I just knew her name, and that this person was very nice. I asked for both telephone numbers, explaining that I lived in Los Angeles, and I needed to speak to this person. I apologized for asking for so much, but told her I was suffering from brain damage, and had lost part of my memory. The receptionist said, "Normally we don't give out employees' home telephone numbers, but because you live so far away, and because of your problem, I'm going to give you the telephone number of each one."

I thanked her much, pleased with the results I had achieved. My next step was to find out which woman was the lady that I recalled. I had two different telephone numbers and two women with the same name. I was so excited to have been able to recall the name of the lady with the blue wedding dress and her employer. It was important to me to communicate with her, to see if what I remembered was true. Was she the lady that married my brother René???

That day I was too exhausted to research the Sarah Bouline I remembered. David entered my office at home, and I told him what I was doing.

"It's fine to get some of your memory back, but you should continue your research tomorrow," David said. "You look very tired."

I followed his advice. I closed November 12th, 1988, thanking my father and God for helping me regain some of my lost memory. Tomorrow, I'm not going to bed until I speak to this Sarah Bouline, I told myself.

November 13th, 1988, I woke up early to make the call. I dialed the first number, listened to the telephone ring, but no one answered. I dialed the second number, and once again got no response. I tried all morning without any positive results.

Because of the difference in time, I decided to call back the hospital where these two women worked. If they weren't at home, they might be at work. I spoke with the same receptionist as the day before and she remembered me. She told me that one of the Sarah's was off work for three days and not at the hospital. The other Sarah worked part time in the morning, so I should be able to reach her at her residence. I kept trying the numbers, determined to speak to the woman with the blue wedding dress. It didn't matter how long I had to stay up to make the calls. At two thirty in the afternoon, I finally reached one Sarah. I introduced myself and asked if she remembered me, explaining my injury and how I was recalling information from my first life, which she was a part of. This lady listened to what I had to say, but informed me that she didn't have any idea who I was. She told me about the other Sarah

Bouline who also worked at the hospital.

I thanked her for her courtesy. I was on my way to finding an answer. For some psychological and intellectual reasons, it was very important to me that this past memory on my road to recovery was actually the truth.

At four p.m. Los Angeles time, I called the second Sarah. A lady answered and I told her my story after introducing myself. I asked if she remembered me.

"How are you, Odette Marie? Yes, I do remember you, and René informed me of your accident."

I told her how I had tried to reach her for the last two days and asked her to verify my recollection of the blue wedding dress. I also asked about one of her sisters, a girl my brother, Steven, liked. I also inquired after her mother who had worked with my brother. It was unbelievable. The information I was retrieving was all true and correct. It was confirmed by the real Sarah Bouline. I felt that my brain had won another victory by bringing back that past segment of my life. I had rediscovered one of my sisters-in-law. Before I let her go, I asked for her address, telling her I would like to write her and send a Christmas card. I also invited her to come to Los Angeles. I spent a lot of time, energy, and money making all these telephone calls to Canada, but it was worth it. Sarah gave me her address, and told me that she would like to meet me. After this telephone call, I was so happy. I felt very hopeful about my recovery. I made one more telephone call to my mother in Québec and told her the complete story. I gave her Sarah's telephone number and address and asked that she call her. I told her how kind this person was to me. My mother listened and said that she was happy for me, but I could feel that she didn't know why my memory recovery was so important to me. I felt that she could not understand.

Today, I no longer blame my mother for not comprehending the importance of the five years following my injury. Everything that an injured person lives through and any information retrieved from the past is really a miracle. It takes a tremendous amount of courage and willpower to make your way back from a brain injury. I feel lucky to have been able to fight back. That was my only way to recuperate.

In February of 1986, four years after I awoke from the coma, my brain started to retrieve melodies my father sang. I recalled music and notes first, then I could hear Dad singing, *"Berceuse de Jocelyn."* Twenty-four hours prior to remembering, I experienced terrible frontal lobe pain as my brain recalled these precious musical segments from my first life. I would remember a melody and then my frontal lobe would be calm for a while. Some nights I woke up with other melodies running through my head. The music had not been erased by my brain injury. However, often I could not recall the words to the songs, so I called my mother and my sister, Sylvie, in Québec to ask if I was remembering the music correctly.

One Sunday morning on the telephone, I sang *"Les Enfants Oubliés"* to Silvie and asked her to correct any mistake and remind me of the words I missed. Then I talked to Mom and sang, *"La Madelon and Souvenirs d'un Vieillard."* These were songs my parents sang and taught me when I was very young. It was a big event for me to realize that the frontal lobe was healing. I was amazed that the music I loved most was the last segment my damaged brain cells were able to recall.

CHAPTER 14
BIOFEEDBACK AND OTHER THERAPY

On February 4th, 1985, David drove me to Kyung Ok Hospital to be hospitalized by Dr. Cucumb for my second spinal surgery. That first morning in the hospital, Dr. Maker, Dr. Cucumb's assistant, informed me that I would have a myelogram and a cat scan on my back. In the afternoon, he returned to my room and said the diagnostic tests showed an unstable lumbar spine.

"The surgery has to be done tomorrow for spinal fusion on the left side. The anesthesiologist will come to see you tonight."

"Dr. Cucumb is my primary physician. Will I see him before he does the surgery?"

"I don't know. I haven't seen him today."

I felt that I had lost my primary physician. Was I going to have another back surgery done without seeing the surgeon first? I told Dr. Maker that my boyfriend, David, would be in the waiting room.

"I'll tell Dr. Cucumb to go see him after the surgery."

When David arrived the next morning, I told him I hadn't seen Dr. Cucumb and that I hoped he would be there to do the surgery.

"I'll be in the waiting room, waiting for both Dr. Maker and Dr. Cucumb," David said.

After three hours, Dr. Maker came to tell him I was fine. They had no problems and the surgery went well. When the nurses took me back to my room, David was there. The next morning I asked him to remind me what I had said after surgery.

"You said you were very happy that you made it. You thought the operation was a success, and you were fortunate to see me," David said.

"I brought you some flowers." He smiled and kissed me. On February 14th, Dr. Maker told me, "Odette Marie, I want you to know that you have three choices after you are released from the hospital. First, you can stay in bed for three months. Second, you can wear a body cast all day to be able to walk. Third, you can stay down for eight weeks, then get up for one to two months with your body cast on."

"Could you repeat that slowly? I need to write what you just told me, if I want to remember."

He repeated those choices and I noted them in my notebook. I would not make a decision until I consulted with my daughter and David after I had arrived home.

The next day Dr. Cucumb, showed up in my room. It was the first time since November 19th, 1984, that I had seen him. He informed me that I was going to be released that afternoon. Also, he prescribed a lumbar seat for me.

"What is that?" I asked.

"Because of your severe back injuries, you need orthopedic support. A lumbar seat will keep your back straight and take some strain off your muscles. You must have this type of support to protect your back, Odette Marie, this is a medical need. Also, just for your information, the best car to provide this type of support is a Volvo. My best friend has one. The seats are designed to provide lumbar and orthopedic assistance."

Before he left, Dr. Cucumb told me he wanted to see me in his office at the beginning of March. He set up a March 5th appointment and said that I was to call Dr. Maker and make an appointment with him for the same day. "You will see both of us," Dr. Cucumb explained. "By the way, how are you getting home?"

"I'm going to call David to come to get me," I said.

Dr. Cucumb left my room without telling me if he did do the surgery on my back with Dr. Maker. He acted strange. His personality was entirely different. Was it because my injured brain was finally able to cope with the libido part, and I had refused to let him use me sexually? Was it because I refused to share an apartment with him between the city where he lived and Thousand Oaks? Or, was it because the last time I saw him at his medical clinic, I told him about David? As his patient, I felt left in the dark; abandoned by my primary physician.

On March 5th, Arlene drove me to see Dr. Maker, Dr. Cucumb, and Dr. Grate. My appointments were eleven o'clock with Dr. Maker, two-thirty with Dr. Cucumb, and three-thirty with Dr. Grate.

"For the time being," Dr. Maker said, "I'm pleased with the results."When I left the exam room, Dr. Maker's secretary gave me a note which read:

11:08am - Odette Marie Kuhlman:
Please call Dr. Cucumb's office
before you leave our office.

When I called Dr. Cucumb's office, the receptionist said, "Dr. Cucumb doesn't want you to come to his office at two-thirty because he can't do anything more for you."

"How can you say that he can't do anything for me when you don't even know why I'm supposed to see him?

"Dr. Cucumb mentioned that you see a neurologist in Thousand Oaks."

"I saw a neurologist one time in 1984 in Thousand Oaks. Dr. Cucumb was apparently the surgeon during my last back surgery on February 5th at the Kyung Ok Hospital. Why don't you tell Dr. Cucumb that I'm not allergic to him. He can see me as a doctor."

"One minute, please."

Dr. Cucumb now took the telephone receiver and said, "Odette Marie, there are two reasons why I don't want you to come here. First, I sent all your records to your neurologist in Thousand Oaks, and second, I can't do anything more for you. Also, I'm not allergic to you."

"I have an appointment with Dr. Grate in San Gabriel at three thirty this afternoon, would you please give me his telephone number?"

"One minute." He came back on the telephone and gave me Dr. Grate's telephone number. I told Dr. Cucumb that I still had pain in my face and didn't know what to do about it. He gave me the name of a Dr. Anthony Fajita, referred by Dr. Maker.

"I don't know him, but if Dr. Maker referred you there, it's because this doctor can help you." Dr. Cucumb said.

After seeing more doctors and dentists who told me that the pain would probably be with me for life, I was completely frustrated. The dentist David recommended, Dr. Matsunaga, thought I should wear a splint for my jaw problem. Finally, I was referred to a chronic pain clinic. I knew that the doctors thought my pain was all in my head, a neurotic complaint, but they were wrong.

I was supposed to stay in bed for three months after the surgery, but I got up with my body cast and sought out help. Pain covered the complete right side of my face. At one point during this time, in frustration, Arlene took me back to Dr. Cucumb's office. When his secretary saw me in tears, she said, "Please wait one minute. Dr. Cucumb will be right with you."

When he entered the exam room, he shook my hand, acting very removed. I explained my problems again, and told him I knew that the doctors thought I was crazy.

"Odette Marie, I'm going to send you to the best *TMJ* doctor in the world. One thing for sure, everything is perfect in your head. The problem is not in your mind. For now, you're my patient. When you feel better and are no longer my patient, I'll see you as my girlfriend. I'll be able to continue loving you."

"I just want this pain to go away. I see you as someone special because you told me how you rescued me, that you saved my life. I need to be free of pain. Nothing else."

When I saw Dr. Maker again on April 10th, he said the fusion looked perfect. However, the central nerve (*sciatic*) could take up to five years before it returned to normal. He said I could start to swim and go in the spa, but I must wear the lumbar brace for one more month.

On April 12th I saw Dr. Vigil, D.D.S., in Alhambra, who said, "I want you to see a doctor for chronic pain. I believe this is very important. My secretary is making an appointment for you with Dr. Blackship.

I saw Dr. Blackship on April 22nd at the clinic for chronic pain, and he told me, "I'm going to give you one prescription. Don't take any other pills, only these, three times a day. I"m also going to send you for therapy called *biofeedback.*

He set up an appointment and gave me a business card with the name and address.

I'll take the pills that you prescribe and I'll go to biofeedback, but I won't see your psychiatrist," I said. "I already see one every week and I'm pleased with him." On April 26th, I went to Hollywood for biofeedback therapy. The clinician, Tanya, was a warm person, extremely nice. We enjoyed talking. She took me to a room where there was a display attached to a keyboard and a few monitors connected together. Tanya explained the devices of biofeedback that we would use, then attached a monitor to me via a wire electrode cord taped on my finger and the front of my head. There was no pain at all. Sometimes, she would type data on the key board and have me breathe. I wasn't allowed to talk when I was being treated using this instrument. I came into the biofeedback lab with physical pain, and I went out of there with the same pain. Tanya wanted me to have biofeedback therapy three times a week. But, it did not provide relief. It didn't matter how many hours I spent there. At the end of six weeks, I informed the clinician that I was considering stopping this type of therapy because of the negative results.

"It might be very good for some people," I said, "but for what I'm concerned about, I believe biofeedback isn't appropriate for me."

"Give it more time," Tanya said. "It is going to help you."

I agreed to go back for one more week.

By May, I was more frustrated. I'd had enough of this training and learning process.

"I don't need to have any electronic instrument attached to me to breathe. I can do it on my own," I told Tanya. "I don't feel changes regarding my facial pain, neck, arm and finger pain. The pain is persistent. Do you have something else that I can try? I need some relief."

"Let me introduce you to Marvin," she said. "He's in physical therapy. Maybe he can do something for you." She called Marvin and asked him to come into the biofeedback lab. Tanya and I continued talking together until Marvin was available. During our conversation I learned that Tanya was Dr. Blackship's sister.

"Why don't you have the same family name?"

"Because I'm married."

This raised some questions with me. "Is Dr. Blackship the owner of this clinic?"

"He is co-owner," she said.

Our conversation was interrupted when Marvin arrived and I went with him to the physical therapy department. He talked to me about a *Tens Unit* and I informed him that I had a *Tens Unit* at home, but it did not help much.

"Maybe you aren't using it correctly. Let me teach you how it works." He began by connecting the electrodes with a generous amount of captor gel.

"I believe I am wasting my time here," I said. "I have a *Tens Unit* with electrodes that use only water. It is very effective and cleaner to use. Can you offer me any other therapy?"

"No. But if you come here after you see Tanya in biofeedback, I can let you use the Tens here and be sure that you use it correctly." I agreed to see him one more time on May 29th. After my biofeedback and physical therapy sessions, I informed Tanya that I would complete the week of biofeedback and that would be the end. I didn't see any changes at all regarding the pain. I took more pain pills and I used the *Tens Unit*, but the pain persisted. These two items just put me to sleep. The pain was tenacious.

"But it'll take more then seven weeks for you to learn how your body functions," Tanya said.

"I know my pain, and I know my body more than any of you. I'll try acupuncture after biofeedback, and if I still have pain, I'll suffer."

I was very discouraged.

Before I left, Marvin gave me his business card.

"Marvin gave me one of his business cards," I told Tanya. "His last name is also Blackship. Is he related to Dr. Blackship?"

"He is his son," she said.

I stared at her. "Marvin is Dr. Blackship's son, and you are Dr. Blackship's sister, and you all work together. Are you an owner of this clinic too?"

"Yes. You've got it right."

"This is quite a family business."

Tanya said nothing else about the family business. "I'll see you tomorrow."

"Yes, I'll come tomorrow probably for the last time. I'm not pleased with the results. I also have an appointment with Dr. Blackship tomorrow."

I left the building hardly believing what a racket they had going. When I asked Tanya how much I owed for the seven weeks of biofeedback therapy and the two times I saw Marvin in physical therapy, she was curt.

"I don't have the bill with me, and it isn't important. Your insurance will pay for it," she responded.

"Even if my *health insurance* will pay for the treatment, I would like to know how much it is. After all, I pay the premium for this *health insurance.*"

"I'll send you a copy of the bill in the mail," she said.

Later that afternoon, I kept my appointment with Dr. Blackship, the head of the pain clinic. He and another doctor came into the exam room. The other doctor looked at me and asked, "What happened to you?" I didn't have time to answer him before Dr. Blackship interrupted.

"Don't question her. I don't want to hear the story anymore. It's very complex."

Dr. Blackship then became very aggressive, accusing me of imagining my pain.

"Sunday, I suffered from pain all day and night," I said.

"You see, pain doesn't kill anybody," he said.

"I called your office and they gave me your emergency telephone number to ask you what I could do to get relief from the pain. You never returned my telephone call. I called another doctor, and I went to the emergency hospital to get a pain shot. I just did what the doctor told me to do. After twenty-two hours of pain, something had to be done."

"You see, you didn't die," Dr. Blackship said coldly. "I'm not going to go to your home to cure you. All your doctors have done too much for you. Personally, I don't feel sorry for you, and I won't go to your home."

"I never invited you to my home and no medical doctor ever came to my home, to cure me, as you say," I responded. I was boiling mad to hear a medical doctor, who thinks he's someone superior, speak to a patient like that. I had to tell him what I thought and I made no bones about it. "I don't believe that it's normal that my daughter, at seven years old, and now ten years of age, has to vacuum the floors, cook her own meals, and do her laundry, because I can't do it. I have too much pain in my face, neck, arm, finger, back, leg and toes. I have pain. Can you understand that?" I said.

"If you love her like you say, why don't you get up and do the work. I believe that you don't love her as much as you say," he responded.

"I hope with all my heart that some day you fall down a canyon and have to seek help. Or maybe I could push you out the window and see how injured you would be, and how you would handle it. As you say, *"pain doesn't kill people."* My angry response didn't stop him.

"There are people who have worse pain than you from things like cancer."

"Dr. Blackship, I'm not responsible if people suffer from cancer, and there is nothing I can do for them. I have plenty of pain, starting with my brain damage. I can't write well anymore, I can't read. I don't understand the meaning of what I look at. On top of that, I've had two laminectomies and an inner ear operation. Of course, I don't have cancer, so you don't care about the pain I'm suffering from."

Dr. Blackship looked at me and said, "Listen to me. Nobody dies of pain. You didn't die when you called me for the pain that you had." He stopped and then asked, "Where is God? Do you see God?"

"God is inside of me. I don't see him, but I know he is there," I said.

"You don't have brain damage," Blackship smiled. "You're very normal."

"I used to be president of two companies, I had a television talk show in Canada, and I was a television producer here in Hollywood before my accident. But now, I don't remember anything about the language or about my work. Friends have to tell me who I was, and what I was doing."

"Because you don't want to. If you wanted, you could do it."

"I'm wasting my energy and time with you. You've used me financially by sending me to your sister for biofeedback, and to your son for physical therapy. You are co-owner of this pain management group. It was one way for you and your family to make money. The female psychiatrist that you wanted to send me to, that I refused to see, is she your grandmother?" I asked.

Dr. Blackship asked me, "Where is your pain now?"

"Dr. Blackship, I will please you by telling you that I do not have any pain now and I only want to get out of here."

"You see, that proves something." He stood up, and left his office. The other doctor looked lost in the argument between Dr. Blackship and me.

I was so angry after going to this clinic. This (supposedly) chronic pain doctor was not professional at all. He was not even human. A pig in a field would have been more polite than Dr. Blackship. I would never understand or even try to understand why he spoke to me like he did. I found it sad that I had to deal with a medical doctor like him.

As I drove back home on the freeway, I started thinking. I decided that if the pain was mental like Dr. Blackship was saying, I shouldn't have any problem painting the walls in the garage. When I got home, I prepared to start. I took a gallon of paint, opened it, mixed it, then walked toward the first wall. The first thing that happened was that I dropped the gallon of paint on the garage floor. The wall didn't get painted that day. Instead, the garage floor was completely covered with gray paint. I wiped up the floor to be sure it was clean everywhere. When David arrived home, I asked him if he could buy more paint. I explained what I had done accidently.

"Maybe it's better if you don't paint at all, Odette Marie," David said.

I insisted that he buy the paint. I needed one more chance, I wanted to prove to myself that I was able to do it. One week later, I did what I needed to do. I started painting and completed the garage walls. I was very proud of myself. Doing this work was important to me. Every day for a period of a week after painting, I would take my shower and go to bed. I was incapable of doing any other kind of work. From my little finger to the shoulder I had no strength, and I had a tremendous amount of facial pain. I just knew that something was wrong. But what? I was taking aspirin with codeine every four hours.

One evening, I talked again with David about my experiences with orthodontists. He advised me to go back to Dr. Matsunaga, which I did.

Together with two other specialists, Dr. Norman Nagel, orthodontist, and Dr. Scott Bennion, oral and maxillofacial surgeon, they recommended that wearing braces might save my teeth and eliminate the facial pain. "There is no guarantee," he said, "But, you won't lose your teeth. There is a strong possibility that all your pain will go away."

Before I had the braces put on, I went to see Dr. Edmunds to get his opinion. He advised me to go ahead with the braces because I wouldn't lose my natural teeth. "You should take a chance that everything will work for you," he said. "The point is to save your natural teeth."

After this recommendation from my neurologist, Dr. Edmund, I decided to have the braces put on. After all, I had nothing to lose at this point by trying something new. On March 2nd, 1988, Dr. Nagel put braces on my upper and lower teeth.

Every month following that day, I would go to his office to get the rubberbands changed, and the braces tightened. During the first year of this new cure, I went to the emergency hospital only one time for a pain shot. In December of 1989, the upper braces were removed and I wore a retainer for six months. In April, the lower braces were removed. Since then I haven't had any more jaw and denture pain.

I am grateful with all my heart to Drs. Matsunaga, Bennion, and Nagel. They saved my natural teeth and freed me from myo-facial pain disfunction.

CHAPTER 15 - ON THE ROAD TO RECOVERY

In August of 1985, Dr. Maker informed me that because I was still complaining of severe pain, particularly on the right side of my body, I had two choices. I could choose to take stronger medication for the pain or try another pain clinic. Going to another clinic would entail a six-week hospital stay where different forms of therapy would be used; acupuncture, psychiatry, and physical therapy. Neither choice appealed to me. I was already seeing a psychiatrist and I had begun acupuncture treatments at a clinic close to my home.

Because I didn't wish to take pain medication for the rest of my life, I asked Dr. Edmund's opinion, and he agreed with Dr. Maker, that a pain clinic might provide some relief. So I made an appointment with Dr. Winer, a neurosurgeon, to find out more and to be evaluated.

We spent well over an hour and fifteen minutes just going through all my old records. His recommendations were that I stay at the Baie Bleue Hôtel close to the pain clinic so I could get acupuncture treatments, use a different kind of *Tens Unit*, and try new medication. Dr. Winer wanted to see how I would react to high doses of antidepressants, while making sure I took all the medication. He thought that I was psychologically disturbed at that time, a condition caused by the brain injury.

He recommended that I make arrangements to go into their structured outpatient pain unit program to work with their entire multi-disciplinary, inter-disciplinary pain team for physical therapy, group psychotherapy, relaxation therapy, audiogenic imagery, and the rest of the program.

The physician gave me a booklet explaining the clinic. They were in their 30th year with the evolution of this pain team. I was also introduced to the accountant of their establishment to discuss how these six weeks of treatment could be paid for. I discussed the plan with David and Véronique, and also with my lawyer because I didn't know if my health insurance would pay for that treatment at the time.

I was not sure if I wanted to go to this pain clinic, but if I decided to go, how would I pay? My lawyer suggested that we give them a lien against the lawsuit with the State of California if my health insurance didn't cover the expenses. So I contacted my insurance first and was informed by the agent that the company would not pay because the insurance program did not cover brain injury even if the damage was created by the accident. As far as the insurer was concerned, any injury to your head was mental. Their plan covered only a maximum of 500 dollars per year for what they considered mental problems. They refused to acknowledge that I was suffering from a physical injury caused by an accident.

"Odette Marie, give the pain clinic a lien on your lawsuit against the State of California as I suggested earlier," my lawyer told me.

I agreed with that in his office, but when I returned home and thought about it, it seemed too scary. What if I lost the lawsuit against the state? Who would pay the 12,000 dollars to the pain clinic? I thought it unfair that I paid 6,000 dollars a year for health insurance for premiums myself and the insurer refused to cover my medical expenses.

In the meantime, I started acupuncture treatments with Dr. Howler in Westlake Village. I went there for approximately a month and a half, one day a week. I found the needles that the physician inserted in the skin very painful, but I swore to myself and to my dead father, that I would continue to get treatment to see if it would be the cure I had been looking for.

Dr. Howler, the acupuncturist, was very professional and a good human being. I rarely saw a physician of this high quality. He informed me the first time that I met him that after a certain period of acupuncture treatment, we could tell if I would respond. If the pain persisted, I should try something else. He was so honest, it was easy to speak to him. I felt that he understood my pain.

My daughter and I swam and used the spa every day. I had a lot of difficulty, but I could move my legs and arms in the water. That was important to me. Instead of using the car to go to the recreational park, we walked there.

I was taking care of my home the best I could. I tried not to feel sorry for myself. I did everything possible to forget the pain. I invited friends over for dinner. I worked in my office at home. I studied the French and English languages, in an effort to regain my former knowledge. I was determined to get back to the way I was before the accident, and I wouldn't miss one day of physical exercise. Mentally, I refused to be handicapped. When I couldn't open the refrigerator door with my right hand without difficulty, I got the refrigerator door changed.

In September of 1985, I informed Dr. Winer that I wouldn't be attending the pain clinic program. Even though I paid for health insurance, I had no easy way to pay the cost of the clinic.

One day in October, while I was swimming, I suddenly got very dizzy and my stomach seemed upset with severe heart burn. A lady helped me out of the water, and went to get a physician. Dr. Johnson arrived, examined me, and said that I was dehydrated.

"What are you telling me?" I asked.

The physician said, "You don't have enough circulation to your brain, that is why you are dizzy and sick. "Did you take any medication before going to the pool?"

I told him that I had taken pain pills. He suggested that they may be part of the problem. Then the lady called David to come and get me. Dr. Johnson told him to give me lots of water and to get plenty of rest.

At an October appointment, Dr. Cucumb told me that my sciatic nerve was "permanently damaged," and he would discuss it with Dr. Maker. There was no cause for pain other than my brain injury. As I was driving home, I wondered if I was going crazy. Did I imagine the pain? Where was it coming from? I only knew that I broke dishes by dropping them on the floor, I cut my finger so often with a knife while trying to cut food, and couldn't arrange a drawer. I felt that a person didn't have to be very intelligent to see that I had physical damage in my right arm. My pain was not all psychological.

At night I'd go to bed and pray to my Dad, asking him to help me stay together. I felt so lost, and knew my father was the only one who understood what I was going through. I believed so much in him. He had to help me to get through this stage of my life.

The following December, I began acupuncture therapy again. This time it was for neck pain. The treatment did help me to relax, but the pain was always there. In April of 1986, I had another appointment with the neurologist, Dr. Edmunds. I informed him of the physical exercise that I was doing on a daily basis, and acupuncture that I was getting two days a week. I also told Dr. Edmunds that although I'd had two laminectomies, the pain persisted.

"We'll have you take an ***MRI*** test. This will show if something is wrong." He gave me a prescription, and his secretary called the MDI medical clinic to make an appointment for me. When the results of the test were available, Dr. Edmunds told me that there was a problem with the vertebrae fusion in my back. A ***Cat Scan*** was done.

"Odette Marie, the ***Cat Scan*** confirmed what the ***MRI*** test showed. You need to have another back surgery. The fusion is broken.

"What?"

"There is failure of the fusion," Dr. Edmunds said. I was very afraid of another back surgery, but pleased that Dr. Edmunds had found the problem.

"I must have been right all along," I said. The pain on my right side was really created by the incomplete bone fusion which was pinching the sciatic nerve. "Drs. Cucumb and Maker kept telling me that the pain was created by my muscle contractions, and stress, by psychological causes. I thought all along that they were wrong, but no one would listen."

"You can have the fusion done by another neurosurgeon, and a different orthopedic doctor," Dr. Edmunds said.

I asked him for the results of my tests. Angry, I decided to show Drs. Cucumb and Maker how ineffective they were. They had performed the first two laminectomies, and if they didn't do it right, they should correct their mistake. Dr. Edmunds agreed with me.

I made an appointment with Dr. Cucumb and also called a neurosurgeon, Dr. Sherwood, in Westlake Village, who confirmed that the fusion was broken. He advised me to get the surgery done soon because the damaged bones were pinching the sciatic nerve and I could become paralyzed. I was beginning to question the competence of my former physicians.

On April 24th, 1986, at ten o'clock in the morning, Dr. Cucumb's secretary called me to postpone my appointment that I was scheduled for at three fifteen, and rescheduled for April 30th at three thirty in the afternoon. I was furious, annoyed by Dr. Cucumb's lack of professionalism. I was repulsed because I wanted to see him only to show him the *MRI* and the *Cat Scan*.

On April 30th, Dr. Cucumb looked at them and said, "You were right. Now I know why you have so much pain, every vertebra is diffused. Let me call Dr. Maker right now. He'll look at these tests, and we'll decide when we'll refuse your vertebrae. It must be done soon, because it's dangerous the way it is now. I do not want you to become paralyzed."

After he spoke with Dr. Maker, Dr. Cucumb studied the reports.

"You should stay in bed until we do the surgery. It's very dangerous. You might injure the sciatic nerve more. Dr. Maker will call the hospital to reserve the surgery room. His office will make you a hospital appointment."

I went upstairs to see Dr. Maker and he scheduled the surgery for May 7th. I was very agitated about Dr. Cucumb. For the first time since I was injured, my brain was starting to understand the mistreatment that my primary surgeon had inflicted on me. I told Dr. Maker, "Dr. Cucumb was the first physician I saw when I came out of the coma. He saved my life. He used to drive 80 miles every week to come by my home in Thousand Oaks, telling me that he had to teach me how to make love because I was mentally disoriented. My brain damage had erased my sexual knowledge. According to him, it was best for my brain to let him do what he was doing to me."

Dr. Maker looked at me sympathetically.

"If Dr. Cucumb needed to cheat on his wife, or if he needed sex, he could have gone to bed with someone that wasn't his patient or someone that lived close to where he practices medicine," I said.

"I understand, Odette Marie. I can't understand him sometimes. The same thing happened with his first wife."

"I am going to let you do the surgery only because you did the two previous ones, and the mistakes were caused by both of you."

On May 2nd, my mother called me. After I explained about the surgery, she said she would think of me and pray for me with others in the family. I was very happy to receive her call because I was so afraid.

This third surgery was called Pseudarthrosis. David and my daughter supported me emotionally. On the day of the surgery, David stayed all day in the hospital waiting room. Three hours after the back surgery, Dr. Maker came to see me to tell me that he wanted to go through my stomach to strengthen the fusion from the inside. David refused to let them touch me without knowing exactly what the purpose of this fourth surgery was. He researched this procedure with friends who were doctors and also with a cousin who is a physician.

He asked Dr. Maker, "How many surgeries have you done before through the stomach?"

"I've never done it before, but I've read about it. I know how to do it."

"You're out of your mind. You want to practice on Odette Marie? Is that your way of learning? Odette Marie is going to get a second opinion before she gets something like this done."

David and I realized only one thing. Dr. Maker wasn't happy when we refused him. I left the hospital without going through a fourth surgery.

During my ten days in the hospital, Dr. Cucumb never visited me, but according to his bill, he had assisted Dr. Maker in surgery. Was he afraid of being questioned by David? Was it because my brain was finally beginning to stabilize and he couldn't use me sexually? When I was released from the hospital, I was left home alone with my daughter. After the previous surgery, a home health care nurse had been prescribed for three months. But this time, Drs. Cucumb and Maker had overlooked it and the insurer refused to pay for the service of a nurse because it wasn't prescribed.

Véronique had a girlfriend whose mother was a nurse at Los Robles Medical Center. Marianne explained that she couldn't help me at home but she would get someone else. The same day I talked to her, someone from Livingston Memorial Visiting Nurse Association called me. Marianne had given them my name and they wanted to evaluate my nursing needs. The next morning, a lady arrived at nine o'clock, questioned me, took the names of my physicians, and called them. In the meantime, someone from the nursing association would come to my home every day. They needed a letter from my doctor in order to administer any necessary medications. A week later, Dr. Maker had sent his recommendation to the nursing group stating that I should have some help at least twelve to fourteen hours a day, seven days a week, for a period of three months.

The nurse made my daughter's lunch, helped me to go to the bathroom and take my shower, and cooked our meals. After a month, I was able to lie on the side of my bed, which allowed the nurse to put the plate of food on the floor so I could eat without her help. I lived this way for three months. One of my neighbors was a French Canadian family. Their son, Justin, was the same age as my daughter, and they played together after school and on the weekends. During the time I was bedridden, Lisette and Gaston, Justin's parents, would prepare dinner for us. Véronique would sometimes eat with Justin and bring home good Canadian food for me to eat.

In the evenings, Lisette frequently visit me. She would sit on my bed, and we would talk. She also brought movies to watch during the day. I found out who my true friends were during those dark days of my life.

I didn't return to see Drs. Cucumb and Maker because I no longer trusted them. In June, Dr. Maker's office called to inform me that I could start walking that day. After I had healed enough to walk, I went to the MDI medical group in Thousand Oaks and took more tests to determine if the pseudarthrosis was successful. I was also concerned about Dr. Maker's recommendation for further surgery to strengthen the fusion, so I visited a Dr. Phillip, in Beverly Hills, recommended by a friend of David's.

I was informed that the fusion looked good, and Dr. Edmund and his colleague, Dr. Beldin, said I did not need another surgery. I was very happy. In one day, I got positive opinions from two doctors. Dr. Phillip, after reviewing all my files, agreed that at this time there was no need for further surgery. He did recommend that I wear my back brace whenever I stood, to alleviate pain.

In June, while I was sleeping on my side, I felt my back bone pulling. It wasn't painful, but it felt as if something was out of place. I became discouraged. I had no income. I couldn't go back to work. I had a daughter to raise and my health insurance wasn't paying my medical bills in a timely manner. They waited so long to pay the doctors and hospitals, that the bills were sent to collection and I was being sued for payment. I explained my situation and that I would be able to make a small payment each month, but that was unacceptable. They wanted to be paid immediately. I was so worried about bills, that Arlene suggested I homestead my home. In this way, my daughter and I were protected.

Later on, David asked Véronique and I to move into his home. He was living alone, and he wanted both of us to be with him. We accepted the offer. I called Arlene and asked her to list our townhouse. Arlene did the market analysis, listed our property, and was available every time a broker came with a buyer to see the property. I was still confined to bed, and the nurse was at my home every day to take care of us.

Arlene took care of everything. The property was sold and escrow was scheduled to close August 15th. She arranged for me to rent back until the end of August. She was a true professional. I can never thank her enough for her help and that of my former real estate broker, Coldwell Banker Residential Real Estate.

Dr. Phillip prescribed an exercise tape called *"Prevent Back Pain,"* by Dr. Art Ulene, which I began using as I healed. In September, Véronique and I moved in with David. It was a good feeling to be loved, and to have a man as a father and friend for my daughter. We both enjoyed being with David.

On November 9th, 1986, I took a second **Polytones** test. *This is a type of X-ray* which was *available before the* **Cat Scan** *was developed. Multiple pictures of the spine are taken focusing an 8th* *of an inch apart. It gives a better picture of each area and allows the orthopedist to go through a piece of bone in segments and see if it is healed. It is like a moving picture which shows if the fusions are solid. Even today,* **Polytones** *is still used and is better than a* **Cat Scan** *for spinal fusions.* Dr. Phillip looked at the **Polytones** lumbar results, and said, "There is one vertebrae, number five, that isn't solid. We might have to fuse it from the inside. Now put your body cast on for the next three months. I want to see you next January. I wore the body cast day and night, removing it only to take my shower.

In December, Dr. Phillip suggested that I be hospitalized at the Cedars-Sinai Pain Control Clinic. The director of the clinic, Doctor Letozy, wanted me in the hospital for two to three weeks. Now that David was home with Véronique, I thought that I had nothing to lose by being hospitalized for new treatment. He would go to work, she'd go to school, and they would be together for dinner. I was sure that Véronique would feel secure with David.

In February, I began to work with the physical and occupational therapist every day at the hospital. I discovered when walking on the ramps with side railings that I was not walking properly. The physical therapist noticed that instead of using my complete foot to walk, I was walking only on my toes, and my right foot was distributing my weight on the outside. Only my toes were supporting my body. I hadn't realized it. It took me many, many sessions to relearn how to use my leg muscles, feet and toes properly. I had been walking wrong since January of 1983.

The therapists taught me how to sit down, stand up, lie down, and how to get out of bed. I had a new body in my second life, a fused spine, and I had never learned how to use it. In addition, I was using my previous body wrong since the accident. I had forgotten how to balance my weight. My body was reborn with destroyed muscles and broken bones, without any knowledge of how to use its parts.

Every day, I would learn something new about my broken body. The pain in my back was always there. I showed the physical therapist where I hurt and she took me to an exercise room to lie down on a bed. She asked me to lie down on my stomach but I told her I couldn't because it might defuse my vertebrae. She gave me a pillow to put under my stomach, this way it wouldn't hurt the lumbar back. Then she began to massage my back and push on the bone that I had asked her to touch earlier.

When she was doing the massage on my back, she said, "Odette Marie this is the pelvic bone that I'm touching. It feels like it is upside down. Tomorrow, I'm going to use more pressure. We have to put it back where it belongs."

The next day I got occupational therapy in the morning for an hour, and physical therapy between ten and eleven o'clock. The therapist continued to work on my back. In the same position as yesterday in the exam room, she pressed on the pelvic bone. I felt it moving back to its place.

"Odette Marie," she said, "I just moved the pelvic bone. It was really upside down. How do you feel?"

I stood up and the pain was entirely gone. "I feel great."

"How did the pelvic bone get displaced?" I asked.

She didn't know the answer. We just knew that the bone was not really where it was supposed to be, and I was free of the pain. A cervical pillow for my neck was prescribed which helped support my head. This too brought some relief.

I saw a neuropsychiatrist, Dr. Amour Offvir, every two days during the time I was there. I was able to talk to her about the mental, emotional, intellectual and physical phases of pain I had experienced in the past. She advised me to stay away from the members of my family that hurt my daughter and me when they came to California while I was comatose. I was counseled to report Dr. Cucumb to the Board of Medicine for sexual abuse. She also proposed that I record film and TV shows to see what I remembered. Dr. Offvir was the most kind human being and professional person that I met in that field. She had great understanding and dedication. During the last psychotherapy session I had with her, she said, "Odette Marie, you must have been a genius before your accident to be where you are today."

When I was released from the hospital, I started walking every morning, wearing orthopedic shoes for the right foot, feeling so lucky that I could use my legs, feet and toes again. I could feel my brain cells beginning to work better. The nerves were reconnecting.

I felt so lucky to have met my Jewish boyfriend, David, and so fortunate that he had a cousin who was in the medical profession. It was so auspicious that David had discovered Dr. King Phillip, one of the greatest orthopedist specialist in Southern California. I was grateful that Dr. Phillip had referred me to the Cedars-Sinai Pain Control Clinic.

It took me five years to find a professional orthopedist that knew what he was doing and where to send me for help. In addition, it took seven years for my brain to regain all reconnections. But I did it. Just knowing that it was happening made me feel successful.

I felt that Dad and God had listened to my pleas. I had a second life, another chance with a different body. I had professional help to teach me about every part of me; and I was at the point where repeating what I learned at the Cedars-Sinai Medical Center was my cure. I practiced the movements that I had learned over and over until I memorized the new me.

My next task was to find a cure for my other ailments; facial pain, neck pain, right shoulder, arm, finger, and knee pain. I understand somewhat why the medical profession felt all my pain had a psychological cause, but they were so limited in their thinking. My hope was to find a physician who was smart in a practical way, as well as intelligent.

Every day at home I swam in the pool. At forty-one, I began taking swimming lessons from a man named David Hershman. The physical pain was incredible. I would drop everything I touched and took in my right hand, and I still had right knee pain even if I wasn't swimming with my legs. But I was committed that nothing was going to stop me.

Dr. Phillip injected Cortisone and Xzylocaine to reduce my back pain. After doing a nerve conduction study of my right arm *("F" wave of the right and left ulnar nerve was performed by placing stimulating electrodes at the wrist with pickup electrodes placed over the hypothenar area. The "F" wave was 26.2 millisec on the right and 24.9 millisec on the left)*, Dr. Edmunds diagnosed that the ulnar nerve was trapped. Dr. Phillip confirmed his diagnosis and recommended surgery to correct the problem. A surgery on the elbow to pull the ulnar nerve apart from the bone might remove the pain. But, Dr. Phillip also cautioned, "No one can say if you will regain the strength in your right arm and hand. Your arm will have to be in a cast for approximately three weeks." The surgery was scheduled for August 11th, at Cedars-Sinai Medical Center.

For the last five years, I had complained to Dr. Cucumb, who would tell me the pain was all created from my brain injury. "You are suffering chronic pain," he said. "You are just lucky to be alive. Nothing more can be done."

The first thing that Dr. Phillip asked me was, "Why did you wait so long to get the surgery done? I had to remove one nerve because it was so injured. If you'd had the surgery done earlier, we could have saved this nerve."

"For the last five years I have been complaining about this pain. But, Dr. Cucumb and his colleagues told me that it was just chronic pain, and it was psychological. This is why the surgery had not been done earlier."

He stared at me because my voice had become aggressive. I was filled with frustration and anger over my long search for competent doctors.

"I had to find a physician that knew what he was doing. And, I found you and Dr. Edmunds. Thanks to both of you, I will finally be able to use my arm and my hand . . . I hope."

"Now that this elbow is taken care of, can anything be done about my right knee?"

"We'll talk about it later," Dr. Phillip responded.

I left his office very worried. I was upset at Drs. Cucumb and Maker. The physical damage had been there since 1982, and was repaired by the new orthopedist five years after the injuries had occurred. But I had waited too long because of incompetent physicians. Now I mentioned my right knee pain to this new orthopedist, and the answer I got was, "We'll talk about it later." What is wrong with these physicians? Why don't they listen to their patients?

On the drive home I asked my Dad, in my mind, to continue helping me. I had to discontinue my swimming lessons, so I decided to walk instead. I couldn't allow myself to feel self-pity. Happily, I felt that God had made me incredibly resilient, and I was able to bounce back. Just being alive was the greatest victory.

I continued to take acupuncture treatments for my right knee, but Dr. Howler advised me to have further studies done because it was not helping. With another **MRI**, Dr. Edmunds discovered my problem, an anterior horn tear of the medial meniscus. Orthoscopic surgery could correct it.

I was overjoyed. I knew that the pain wasn't in my head. Dr. Edmunds could not perform the surgery, but referred me to Dr. Mark Deceiving, who recommended Dr. Howler, the acupuncturist, be the anesthesiologist.

Dr. Phillip explained that he could perform the knee surgery, but I was disturbed because he had put me off before. I went along with Dr. Deceiving instead. I had complained of pain, but Dr. Phillip had not listened.

On December 1st, 1987, the surgery was done on my right knee. I talked to Dr. Deceiving and Dr. Howler before I was put to sleep. One more time, my life was in the hands of a surgeon. On Friday, December 4th, I was able to start walking. I walked two miles at first, and following that, I went back to my regular schedule of walking six miles a day.

I was determined to get every bit of my broken body repaired, I had the naivete of a child, thinking that surgery would return my body to the excellent physical condition it once was in. Today, I realize that it was only a dream. The knee surgery was a success. I can drive my car now without using both feet. The elbow ulnar nerve transfer surgery was also successful. When I say successful, I mean I can use these parts of my body now. I still have aches, but nothing like before. In my right hand, the baby finger still has a dull sense of touch, and my right arm where the nerve had been transferred, is very sensitive. But, I can write, I can hold what I take in my hand most of the time, I can hug my daughter and my boyfriend. I'm happy.

I felt that two more injuries needed to be repaired, and I could live with it. I don't know if I will ever be able to accept what I lost since the accident, but I'm not paralyzed. I was on my way back to being free from pain.

On December 7th, I had a followup with the orthopedic surgeon who did the right knee surgery. The inside of my knee was still bothering me. I had pain and could feel something that didn't belong there. My physician prescribed physical therapy at his office.

After spending Christmas vacation in Québec with my family, I started physical therapy as planned. I went to the orthopedist's office for treatment but was disappointed by their lack of professionalism. I felt that I was paying for treatment that I was not receiving. I continued to have some knee pain. The clinic was very crowded, so I decided to get my own exercise bicycle and use it at home.

During this time, a friend of mine told me she thought there was nothing wrong with my knee. "You just get surgery done because you like it, Odette Marie," she said, "I would never let a surgeon touch me that way." When I told Dr. Deceiving about this, he advised me, "Mrs. Kuhlman don't ever lose your self-esteem. You're beautiful. Ignore people that hurt you, and keep your self-esteem."

I took his advice. Since the orthoscopic surgery was done, I do more and more physical exercises. I walk first thing in the morning at five o'clock. At eight o'clock, it's time for me to ride the exercise bike for an hour. It makes me perspire and strengthens my body, maintaining it in good physical condition. I have grown to love exercising. I feel that it's excellent for my brain. It improves my blood circulation and makes me feel my heart, lungs, and muscles are in excellent condition. I get the sensation that I have a lot of willpower, and I'll continue to use it.

Ever since I awoke from the coma, I had difficulty opening my eyes to their normal size. In the morning I would have to hold a cloth dipped in hot water to my eyes. That was the only way to open them. I asked many different doctors about this, but they only said, "Your brain injury affected your eyes. When your brain stabilizes, you will be able to see better."

"But why am I unable to open my eyes all the way? Why is my vision blurry?" I asked.

That is normal for a brain-injured person is what I was told.

I tolerated this discomfort until 1987 when I was referred to a plastic surgeon, Dr. Guttman. On my first visit I explained my problem and asked if something could be done.

After taking pictures and examining my eyes, Dr. Guttman said, "You need eyelid surgery. I'm going to remove all the fatty tissue, and then you will be able to open your eyes. You won't have anymore problems."

When I inquired if my health insurance would cover this type of surgery, and if I could have a written quote, Dr. Guttman referred me to Michael, an insurance specialist in his office. Surgery was scheduled for November 4th, 1987, in Dr. Guttman's office and he assured me that there would be no problem. I was very scared . . . afraid to lose my vision.

"Don't worry, you'll be all right," he said.

After the surgery, I visited the doctor regularly because now I was unable to close my eyes. Many times, my daughter and David would come into my bedroom to talk to me. I would get upset that they woke me up. They would say, "You weren't sleeping. Your eyes were open!"

"I was asleep," I would said, puzzled.

At one point, David and Véronique decided to take pictures of me in my bed every time they would enter the room. They wanted to show how I slept with open eyes since the eyelid surgery. I took these pictures to the plastic surgeon, but he assured me that it was normal after the surgery, and that my eyes would close with time.

As I left his office, I spoke with two of his employees, and one other patient. This is when I learned that Dr. Guttman's specialty was breast surgery. I couldn't believe it! He never told me he wasn't a specialist in ophthalmic plastic surgery. He had performed a procedure that I didn't need. My eyes now felt as though I had sandpaper on them. I had great difficulty opening or closing them. Furthermore, if I needed to cry, I had no tears.

It wasn't until 1991 when I was referred to Dr. Bruce Ford, an ophthalmic plastic surgeon, that I was told that *"ectropion reconstruction of left and right eyes"* needed to be done. Dr. Ford took tissue from behind my ears and grafted it under my lower lids. After that, I was able to close my eyes for the first time in four years.

Two more eye surgeries had to be performed because of my deficient tear production, *"Keratitis Sicca."* My life was one surgical nightmare after another.

Because I had tremendous pain that started on the top of my right shoulder and moved down through my arm, I was limited in its use. Dr. Phillip in Beverly Hills, whom I visited for the problem, gave me a prescription for physical and occupational therapy.

On May 3rd, I went to Los Robles Medical Center for occupational therapy. I learned how to move my arm with weights, how to do circles, arm lifts and shoulder touches. In addition to the 30 minutes of occupational therapy, a physical therapist would massage my back, shoulder and neck with cream. I had a great deal of discomfort in my shoulder and neck.

While my therapy was beginning to help me, I was approached by a woman from the office, "Mrs. Kuhlman, we have some problems. Your health insurance company is refusing to pay the bills that we sent them for the last six weeks. We can't continue giving you occupational and physical therapy until they pay."

"Where did you send the bills?"

"To Fresno. If you want to pay personally, you can continue to receive treatment. Otherwise, we'll have to discontinue until the medical charges are paid."

"I'm not going to pay the bill myself. It costs me 6,000 dollars a year to be insured with that insurer. I'm going to call their office to find out when a check will be sent to you."

That was the last day of occupational and physical therapy that I received, because I had refused to pay personally. The hospital was paid ten months later by the health insurance. During all that time, I was in pain. The insurer didn't care.

During the ten months the hospital was waiting to get paid, they would send me a bill the first week of every month asking me to pay the bill. Otherwise, they would turn the bills over to collection. I was at a point where I didn't care anymore. I'd had enough of this system between the health insurance company, doctors, and hospitals. The patient that needs medical treatment is only a puppet to the insurer. In my native Québec, these problems would not have existed.

Sustaining brain damage in the accident destroyed me as a person. I believe that brain damage is the most devastating physical injury a person can suffer. I suffered not only *cerebral injury*, but also *edema*, which is the collection of fluid in the brain tissue causing swelling. I always thought that I had a brain surgery done, because I could feel a scar on the back of my head. But in 1983, I learned from Dr. Cucumb that the cut was where my head opened when I hit the tree, and the brain damage was in the right *frontal lobe.*

Three months after I awoke from the coma, I needed to eat sugar. My brain craved it. I had lost my sense of taste and my sense of smell. The only thing that my brain knew was sugar. I would be going to one of my many doctors' appointments and I would ask my driver, Arlene, "Can we stop somewhere to buy sugar? I must have sugar. I need it now."

She would go buy a box of donuts and, during the 50 miles trip from Thousand Oaks to Torrance, I would eat the entire box. After I ate all of this sugar, I would feel relaxed and my brain was satisfied. For the first five years, I fed my brain. I didn't care about any other kind of food because I couldn't taste anything. From 1983 though 1986 I gained thirty pounds just by feeding my brain what it needed.

I was never obese before my accident. I wore a size 4 previously, and now I was into 10s and 12s. I had gained too much weight. Dr. Edmunds checked me for diabetes, but informed me that following a brain injury, it was normal for my brain to crave a great deal of sugar.

My orthopedist, Dr. Phillip, advised me to lose weight, up to 15 pounds below my normal weight. "Your vertebrae can't carry too much weigh. I would like you to weight not more than one hundred and thirty pounds," he said. I began to substitute honey for sugar and drank a lot of water to fill my stomach. I knew I must lose the weight. I also ate tapioca pudding made with dry milk and honey.

I tried to remember that procrastination would kill my inspiration. Every morning, I would remind myself. It took me a certain period of time to reach my weight of one hundred and thirty pounds, but I did it by changing my eating habits. That was over five years ago and I've never gained any weight back.

After becoming aware of why my brain wanted so much sugar, I had to use my willpower to control it. I believed I needed to stay thin. Eating began to make me feel guilty. I continued my walking, six miles a day, talking to my father and God, asking both of them to continue supporting me. I realized that when I had healed, I wanted to help other people that suffered from brain injury. Without Dad and God, I would never have been able to fight back. That was my way of surviving.

Many mornings at five o'clock I would have preferred to stay in bed where it was warm and secure, but I felt I couldn't do this. Instead, the moment I woke up I would say a prayer to Dad in my mind, and force myself to get up. I had to do it.

After a while I became addicted to walking. It became a necessity to my body, like brushing my teeth, washing myself, or eating. Life was difficult at that time, and I didn't want to get addicted to prescription pills. I had to find a way to stop taking medication, but still get relief from pain. Physical exercise became my principal device.

During my walk in the mornings, I would try to memorize the names of the streets, how to spell them, and how to pronounce them. My goal was to remember. To know exactly where I was.

Similar names confused me. I had difficulty learning the difference between Lindero Canyon Road and Lake Lindero Drive.

At the main street, Thousand Oaks Boulevard, it was difficult to know if I should turn left or right.

A friend, Hypocrita, began to walk with me. She would pronounce the name of each street, and I would repeat it after her. I tried to learn how to spell these street names. After many months of pronouncing and learning how to spell the names of each one, I told David and Véronique one night that I had to go walk because I really felt that my memory was becoming more stable. I wanted to check out the street names and see if I remembered correctly.

"Why don't you wait until tomorrow morning when Hypocrita will be with you?" David said. "You already walked your six miles today. Don't you think that's enough?"

"Sweetheart, if you knew how important it is for me to check my recent memory tonight, you would feel differently. If I don't do it now, I'm afraid that I'll forget. Don't worry about me. Let me go see these street names, and I'll be right back."

I left home with a lot of inspiration. My insides felt positive about remembering the information. After all, I had been walking on the same roads for eight months.

Cape Horn Drive, the street that I lived on, I remembered. Lake Lindero Drive I got wrong, I thought that it was Lindero Canyon Road. I could picture Reyes Adobe Road, but I could not pronounce it. I had completely forgotten Middle Crest Drive. It was frustrating, but I wasn't discouraged. I believed that with time my brain would work harder to remember these data.

David was so worried about me walking alone that night, that he drove his car on Thousand Oaks Boulevard to see where I was. I felt that he was checking on me. He drove his car near the sidewalk, put the window down, and asked me to let him drive me back home.

"David I can't do that to myself. I must walk back home. I was really able to recall some street names, sweetheart. I'll be home very soon."

David insisted. "Are you sure you want to walk?"

"Yes, I must walk back home."

When I arrived home, I asked David why he was checking on me. "Didn't you think I could remember my way home?"

David responded in such a loving and delicate manner."Odette Marie, you had so many back surgeries that I was afraid you would be tired. You already walked six miles today. If you do too much, you're going to hurt yourself."

The next morning when Hypocrita joined me for our walk, I told her about the night before. Memorizing one street to be sure that I wouldn't get lost when I went walking alone was one of my goals. I started to memorize streets that I should take. Many times, I felt afraid. I was not sure if I could walk further by myself without forgetting my way back home. In my heart, I told myself if I didn't try it, I'd never get it. I forced myself to walk twice a day. And, I accepted that David checked on me. I would tell him, "Darling, I'm going to walk alone, if I'm not back in an hour and a half, would you come to see where I am?"

For another six months, I walked with Hypocrita in the morning. Every night I covered the same distance to learn how to pronounce and spell the name of each road. It took me fourteen months of hard work to bring my memory back.

One day, I finally trusted myself and tried a different route. When I arrived home, my brain throbbed with life and activity. I was feeling so much brain power that I could have built a castle. I followed my route in the car before David arrived home from work and clocked the distance at eight miles. My stubbornness made me feel glorious. I had travelled this distance with the help of no one but myself.

In the morning, I always walked six miles, and in the afternoon, I would walk the new way of eight miles. At dinner time, I was so exhausted physically, that I would serve dinner to David and Véronique, and then go to bed, usually by six thirty.

I could feel my intellectual power coming back, and my digestive capacity and relaxing processes were excellent. Walking became a muscle relaxant. I didn't have to take capsules anymore to relax. Exercising was going directly to action on my blood brain barrier, allowing more oxygen in.

I had to take control of my destiny, and nobody else could do it for me. That was my responsibility. Now, I walked completely alone every day that God let me have and I thanked him and Dad for all the courage and determination. Before my brain could retrieve past events, I would have terrible *frontal lobe* area pain, and I had a feeling like nerves were getting reconnected. The collection of fluid in my brain tissue which had caused the swelling was diminishing. After three to four hours of **brain frontal lobe** pain, I was able to clear thoughts and I started feeling more stable on my feet.

I want to share with you that I believe that I was successful only because I didn't lose persistence. I set goals and I reached them only through hard work. I had been unfortunate to grow up feeling unloved and unwanted by my mother, but what saved me was the love of my father and the self-worth I was born with. I refuse to be a failure.

Rarely do we take time to look at our legs, arms, fingers, our entire body and say, "Thank you for what you have given me, God. I love and appreciate what I have, and I don't want to lose it." I don't remember ever having taken the time before my fall to do this. I took life for granted. Since I came out of the coma, I thank God every morning for what I possess.

CHAPTER 16 - JUSTICE

During the time of my physical and occupational therapies, and surgeries, I also had to deal with attorneys. One lawsuit was filed against the State of California, as I mentioned earlier, plus a second lawsuit was filed against my health insurance company because they refused to cover medical expenses for treatment that I needed. The first, for personal injury and wrongful death, had been filed by my mother and my sister, Simone.

In early March, 1983, while I was staying at my friend Dustin's home, I received a telephone call in Ottawa from the attorney, Mr. Anson, in Los Angeles. He introduced himself and said. "Mrs. Kuhlman, you must come to Los Angeles as soon as possible. You have ninety days to take action against the State of California regarding the accident that your husband, your daughter and you had in Angeles Crest Canyon. We need you here to sign the lawsuit papers."

"What are you talking about? I never filed a lawsuit."

"Your sister took care of engaging us when you were still in a coma."

"Why don't you ask her to sign?"

"She can't sign for you. You're alive and able to sign. Just come to Los Angeles to my office, I'll explain everything. Let me give you my telephone number. When you arrive in Los Angeles, give me a call and I'll tell you how to get here, but it must be soon."

At the time, I was still confused and had a difficult time following what he told me.

"The lawsuit depends on your signature and we've already had an extension from the court."

"As soon as my friend Dustin arrives home, I'll ask him to call you," I said. "I can't go back to Los Angeles without him." Mr. Anson agreed to communicate with Dustin.

Dustin arrived around midnight and I gave him the attorney's telephone number. I explained what I knew about this lawyer.

"I'll call him tomorrow from my office," Dustin said. "It's nine o'clock in Los Angeles and his office is closed, I'm sure."

The next day Dustin told me that he had contacted Mr. Anson and we had an appointment with him in Los Angeles.

We met Mr. Anson on March 24th and after I had told him I could not read the agreement he had prepared, he gave it to Dustin. Then he explained to me what was written. His fee would be thirty-three and one-third percent of the sum recovered. If settled before trial, or through arbitration or other means, it would be forty percent.

When we left his office, I spoke to Dustin.

"If I go to Court and they ask me how the accident happened, my answer will be, I don't know. I don't even know where we were. It's awful not knowing anything about the accident, or understanding this lawsuit."

"Odette Marie," Dustin said, "This lawyer knows what he's doing. Let him. You might become a millionaire."

Later, when we were back in California, I had just hung up the telephone from a conversation with a friend when the phone rang. When I answered, Mr. Anson was on the line.

"Mrs. Kuhlman, I have been trying to call you for the last thirty minutes and your telephone has been busy. You must keep a line free. Don't use your telephone so much. When I need to speak to you, I want this telephone to be free. I can't be waiting like I did this morning," he said.

"I need to use this telephone. I have friends that check on me every day and they call here," I said. "I'm not on the telephone just for fun."

"I don't care why you use the telephone. I want this line to be reserved for me and my employees when we need to talk to you. Get a second line installed if necessary."

I listened to what he had to say, and then hung up the receiver. Who did this lawyer think he was?

When Véronique came back home from school, I told her that she shouldn't use the telephone any longer than necessary and told her what Mr. Anson had said. Véronique wasn't very happy about it. "When Don arrives, *(a friend of the family)* mama is going to ask him what he thinks about this lawyer's request."

During the evening, Don came to visit us and I told him the story about Mr. Anson and the telephone. He suggested that I get a second line installed to please this lawyer. We were talking about a lawsuit of $23 million. Your daughter's and your own health and security are at stake," he said. "Tomorrow I'll call the telephone company and get a second line installed. Don't worry about it. I'll take care of it and I'll buy you another telephone."

On another occasion, before I had my first back surgery done, someone knocked at my front door one afternoon. With great difficulty, I walked to the first floor to see who was there. It was a paralegal from Mr. Anson's firm. She came to see me to get information she needed regarding the suit. She didn't bother to call me first, but just showed up, acting as though it was my duty to be available to her. I answered her questions and showed her the file that she wanted to see. I listened to what she was telling me, and hoped I could do what they wanted. I tried to explain to her that when Mr. Anson called me, he spoke too fast. I couldn't register what he told me. I could remember only through vision. She tried to understand my situation, but said, "Mr. Anson needs these things. He's representing you in a lawsuit against the State of California and the County of Los Angeles."

The following day I received a telephone call from Mr. Anson. He had some important things to tell me.

1. Don't ever get out of your car until the garage door
   is closed. I don't want anyone to see you.
2. Don't work outside in the garden. I don't want
   anyone to see you.
3. Don't remarry.
   (When I asked why not, he told me "When we go to
   court, the judge and jury will feel more sorry for you
   if you're a widow. It's very important in your case that
   you don't change your status. I want you to stay a
   widow until the lawsuit with the State of California
   is settled).
   I told him I would like to have a new husband, that my
   daughter needed a father. He said I could live with someone as long as I wanted, but not to get remarried.
4. Don't speak to anyone about the lawsuit. If anybody asks
   you questions, you don't know the answer.

5. The State of California is rich, and they have somebody watching you.

You must be careful.

When I heard this list, I said I would try to respect his demands, but felt that my daughter and I were prisoners of the legal system. It didn't matter what we were feeling, what we needed in our lives. We had become a business target. This attorney-at-law was going to make money off of my deceased husband's body, off of my daughter, and off of my injuries.

At that time, I was unable to accept the fact that the lawyer was targeting my family's injuries to make money. I felt it was terrible. My question was always the same. Why us? This accident could have happened to anybody.

Mr. Anson knew everything about the accident. He informed Dustin and I that ten people had fallen in the same canyon area. I was the seventh one to fall, and only one young man and I had survived. He knew that John had fallen 1200 feet and that I had fallen 600 feet. It was one of the worst winters for snow in the San Gabriel Mountains, according to what the lawyer told us. There was so much snow, that the people responsible for removal didn't know where to put it. They had decided to push the snow onto the turnout and the public couldn't see where the actual edge of the turnout was. No warning signs were installed to inform the public of the danger and no fence was installed to let citizens know that this turnout was an area where many had been killed.

"There is a ninety percent chance of winning this lawsuit," Mr. Anson said. "If you remember something about the accident, give me a call."

I called him often because I had so many questions. He would never be available, and he would never return my telephone call, but instead, would send a secretary or a paralegal to see me. They would never call before coming and would arrive at my residence expecting me to be there.

At that time, I was living in the past, mentally. They said, "You look so good, nobody would think that you're injured. This doesn't help us. If you were in a wheelchair, if you were paralyzed, people would feel sorry for you."

Constantly, someone from Mr. Anson's firm would come to my home. I had difficulty accepting this even though the paralegal was nice to me. I was at a period where I was trying to face John's death, to understand the drama that I was in, and I was worried for my daughter. These people would come to my home only to talk about money.

One day the paralegal told me, "Mr. Anson has had a miniature mountain built by an architect in San Francisco to bring to court. He wants to show the judge how dangerous this mountain was, and where every victim had been found. It cost him 15,000 dollars to get this done."

I was not impressed.

"Your attorney is a good lawyer, but he's an even better, I should say, an excellent politician. He's friends with all the judges in the State," she said. "They all know him. If he wanted to become a judge, he would only have to make one telephone call."

According to her, his income was larger as a lawyer than it would be as a judge. He was sure to win this lawsuit because of his situation in politics. I'll never forget the day that this paralegal told me, "Mr. Anson will win your case. If it isn't as a lawyer, it will be as a politician."

I let her say what she wanted during her visits and during our telephone conversations. She was only doing her job. But after she would leave my home, I wanted to drop the lawsuit. I'd had enough. I asked one of my friends, who was also an attorney, how I could forfeit from the lawsuit. What did I have to do to make this lawyer stop. At that time, my daughter was the most important person on earth for me. My recuperation was another goal. I couldn't understand how they spoke only of money and business, not considering that, in life, there is more than money to live for.

My friends would tell me, "Odette Marie, John is dead because of the negligence of the people that were clearing the canyon. These people were employed by the State and the County. Your daughter has been emotionally injured, and you're handicapped for the balance of your life. All this created by negligence of these people. Do you understand that? Your daughter is young, she lost her daddy, and I don't see how you can go back to work. So, let your lawyer do his job. You might get something out of this lawsuit."

I would relax until I received another telephone call from them or someone from their office showed up at my door. I was so mad at myself for not being able to be what I used to be. My financial future depended on them. I wanted everybody to understand and to see the brain damage that I was living with.

On November 19th, I had an appointment with another attorney, Mr. Koosch, in Torrance, California. I asked him if he could handle the lawsuit against the State of California. I just couldn't deal with Mr. Anson anymore. I wanted an attorney who was also a good human being.

"I don't work in that field of law," Mr. Koosch answered. "This is an expensive lawsuit and I'm not specialized in this type of suit. But, I can refer you to one of my colleagues."

"Who is that?" I asked.

"His name is Mr. Gaines. I went to law school with him and he specializes in this field." So, Mr. Koosch gave me the name and telephone number of Mr. Gaines.

On November 26th, 1984, I had an appointment with Mr. Anson. David drove me there. I left the meeting with a copy of a general retainer agreement Mr. Anson wanted me to sign. But, on David's advice, I declined. I was going to have this retainer agreement explained to me in detail, and if it was correct, I'd sign it and return it to the lawyer.

The next month, I made an appointment with Mr. Gaines. After explaining the accident and the lawsuit my mother and Simone had initiated, I told him I couldn't work with Mr. Anson. "He never returned my telephone calls, writing letters instead, when he knew that I could not read. Someone from his office always comes to my home without calling first."

Mr. Gaines asked, "What kind of injury did you get from this accident?"

"I was comatose for a period of time, and I have brain damage. When I returned to Los Angeles, I had inner ear and back surgery done, but I'm still in pain."

"Who is your doctor?" Mr. Gaines asked.

"Dr. Ray Cucumb has been my primary physician since he rescued me from the mountain. He told me to tell my lawyer that if you need a witness when we go to court, he will be there and say what you want him to say."

Mr. Gaines asked me again, "What is the name of your doctor?" I repeated Dr. Cucumb's name, and Mr. Gaines said that Dr. Cucumb would probably be our major medical witness.

"But Dr. Cucumb used to drive to my home in Thousand Oaks to teach me how to make love after I came out of the coma," I said.

"He said that it was important for the recuperation of my brain. But my psychiatrists, Drs. Krell and Andreassen, said that Dr. Cucumb was using me . . . that he was abusing me sexually because he knew how injured I was." "Don't talk to anybody about that," Mr. Gaines said. "We'll need this doctor when our case goes to trial; it is important that you don't discuss this with anyone. Now, if you'd like, I'll take this case. It's the type I specialize in."

"Should I inform Mr. Anson that he is no longer on the case?" I asked.

"No. No. I'll send somebody from this office to pick up your files," he said. "If you go yourself, he'll talk you out of it. Let me take care of him."

One more time, my robot-like brain allowed me to go along with what Mr. Gaines was telling me.

"When I need to speak to you about the lawsuit, will you be available?" I asked.

"Yes! don't worry about it. I won't act like your previous lawyer. We'll talk together, I'll answer your phone calls," he said.

"What is your fee to handle this lawsuit?"

"Thirty percent of the total settlement or one-third of those sums collected."

I wanted to have this in writing and he told me that during the coming week, I would receive a Retainer Agreement. This was just before Christmas, and I felt I was finishing the year on a good foundation. I was glad to have a new lawyer, but sad not to have been allowed to go talk with Mr. Anson. I believed in communicating, but this new lawyer didn't want me to.

When I didn't receive an agreement from Mr. Gaines by the first of the new year, I became angry. I wrote him a letter by sound, but he didn't answer. I made telephone calls to his office that went unanswered. Mr. Gaines refused to communicate.

I sent him three letters asking for the agreement, and finally received a letter from him telling me that my letter of May 11th was correct. His fee in this case will be one-third of the total settlement or one-third of those sums collected. The date was July 6th, 1985.

My aggravation over this lawyer's behavior was enormous. It took him six months to send a Retainer Agreement. At that time, I couldn't cope. I felt that if I wasn't suffering from brain damage, these lawyers wouldn't treat me this way. They were taking advantage, and I was as angry at Mr. Gaines as I had been at Mr. Anson. These attorneys had such big egos that they couldn't carry their heads.

On April 14th, 1985, I received a letter from Mr. Gaines informing me that the court had set my case for a mandatory settlement conference on October 11th,1985, at nine o'clock in the morning. It would be necessary for me to attend this conference. Mr. Gaines wanted me to meet him outside of Department "C" shortly before eight o'clock.

The second paragraph of his letter informed me that the trial of my case was presently set for November 18th, 1985, at ten o'clock. He would be in touch with me prior to that time to prepare me for trial, if a settlement wasn't reached at the mandatory settlement conference.

On October 10th, 1985, I received a phone call from Mr. Gaines' office informing me that my lawyer wanted to go to the mandatory settlement conference alone. I stayed home waiting to receive a phone call which never came.

On November 18th, 1985, the scheduled day of the trial, David and I went to the courthouse. Mr. Gaines wasn't there, but had sent one of his young associates who informed us that our trial date had been continued to February 3rd, 1986, at ten o'clock.

While waiting for the trial all this time, all of my medical providers, except one hospital, had accepted taking a lien against my lawsuit in payment for their services. I needed to ask Mr. Gaines if he would prepare lien forms for these providers. I called him many times, but he never returned my telephone calls. I'd finally had enough worrying about the medical bills. Therefore, I decided to write a registered letter to Mr. Gaines.

1/6/86

Dear Sir,

Since I asked you to represent me in the "Kuhlman vs. The State of California," you are ignoring me completely. You, Mr. Gaines, don't give a darn what happens to my daughter and me. The only thing that you care about is your millions of dollars. If I call at your office to speak to you, you never return my telephone call, even if I leave a message. You are either too busy or you don't want to discuss the subject.

Two attorneys, Mr. Koosch in Torrance, and Mr. Hamm in Los Angeles, both told me that it is your job to prepare liens on my case to the medical providers.

*The injuries I'm suffering from are all caused by the accident in the Angeles Crest Canyon. I lost my husband, I lost my health, I lost all income, and I lost my health insurance. My daughter was emotionally injured for a year and a half, etc. Maybe for you that is a joke . . . **BUT NOT TO ME.** I cannot get my husband back, I cannot get my capacity back to go to work, but I can get some of my health back, if you do your job by preparing lien forms for these medical doctors and hospitals who have refused to see me because you won't contact them. If you choose not to prepare the lien forms for the list of names attached, let me know in writing within five days. After this period of time, if I don't hear from you, I will be forced to seek other legal representation.*

Sincerely,

Odette Marie Kuhlman

Mr. Gaines never answered my letter in writing. On January 14th, 1986, he did call me at my residence. He was very angry. The first thing he said to me was, "Mrs. Kuhlman, I received your letter. I've been an attorney for many years and I've never received a letter like that in my entire career. I'm not going to accept this type of letter." I let him say everything that he wanted, and then asked if he would prepare the lien forms.

"Yes, I'll do it," he said. "Ask your doctors to send the forms to my office and I'll prepare them."

That was the end of our conversation. I didn't have any problems after that day. By the sound of his voice, I believe his blood pressure went sky high. Even if my writing was terrible, it didn't bother me. I wanted to be able to continue receiving medical treatments. It was important to me that physicians bills were covered and if it took this letter to make Mr. Gaines respond, it was worth it. I had absolutely nothing to lose by sending him the letter.

On February 3rd, 1986, David and I were again at the courthouse in Los Angeles where we were informed that the trial date had been continued to April 28th, 1986. The court date was confirmed in writing, and Mr. Gaines asked that I meet him outside of Department "C" shortly before eight thirty in the morning. David and I were there as agreed, but my lawyer didn't show up. One of his young associates was present. The trial had been postponed.

On June 18th, 1986, the defendant's lawyer and my lawyer's associate came to my residence to take my deposition. On July 9th, 1986, both lawyers came back to take Véronique's deposition. In August, an investigator from my lawyer's office came to our home to show us pictures of the mountain. Then, in September, the same investigator returned to our residence to pick up Véronique and I to go to Angeles Crest Canyon. This man was absolutely an angel. He was devoted to his job, and polite and considerate toward my daughter and me.

I was informed by my lawyer that the trial had been scheduled by the court for March 11th, 1987 at ten o'clock in the morning. I arrived in court on March 11th to find out that the trial in our case had again been rescheduled, to April 6th, 1987. When I showed up shortly before ten o'clock to meet my lawyer, I found out that one more time the court had reset our trial date for September 28th, 1987, at ten o'clock.

Time after time I went to court as scheduled, but the case would be continued every time it came up for trial. I went to Superior Court in Los Angeles six more times for no reason. It was always rescheduled.

On October 2nd, 1987, I called Mr. Gaines' office to inform him that David asked me to marry him. He wasn't there, but his secretary advised me to speak with another attorney, Mr. Miller. I explained to him that this was the second time David had asked me to marry him and I wanted to do it. Was this all right?

"I'll have to talk with Mr. Gaines about it," he said. "It may be better if you wait until the case is settled."

Between 1983 and 1984, I spent over 53,000 dollars for medical services. If I hadn't paid with cash, the providers would have told me to go to hell because in California, poor legal immigrants don't have free access to medical care; and free medical care is not available to Americans. I managed to cover these medical expenses hoping that one day the insurer would reimburse me.

After I became emotionally and physically impoverished, even though the insurer knew of my accident and knew that medical treatments were very important to my recovery, they didn't care. I felt that all they wanted was to make money off me, take my premium payments, but not honor my medical claims. It caused me great grief during this difficult time. This would never have happened if America had national medical reform like it exists in Québec.

At the time, our neighbor's daughter, Monica, was working for a lawyer in Van Nuys who specialized in punitive damages and bad faith lawsuits. She told David that her employer won many lawsuits against health insurers and recommended that we see Mr. John Bukinshaw.

At the first meeting, I explained the details of the accident the best I could. I told Mr. Bukinshaw that since my husband died, I'd had problems with Orange Health Insurance Company. The insurer refused to pay for many medical bills, and would not allow me to get medical treatment for the brain damage and other physical injuries.

He asked me questions about the physicians that treated me and the kind of surgeries that were done. He also asked about my primary physician. At the time he could see that I was still dizzy and needed to lean on something when I stood.

After answering his questions, Mr. Bukinshaw told me that it looked like I had good cause for a bad faith lawsuit against the insurer. His professional fee would be 45% commission if the case was settled out of court, and 50% commission if we had to go to court. Before our departure from his office, he made another appointment for March 21st, 1986, at three o'clock in the afternoon at his office. He needed some time to look at my file and analyze the case before he decided to take it.

On March 21st, I gave him three boxes containing medical bills and the insurer's correspondence files. During our meeting, I informed him that Dr. Cucumb, my primary physician, would testify for me if necessary.

"I'll let you know my decision after I review the files," Mr. Bukinshaw said. He called me on March 25th and said he needed more time to finish reading the files. "I like what I've read, and I like you, Mrs. Kuhlman," he said. "Be patient."

Our next appointment was postponed to March 31st. On that date, I kept my appointment, but didn't contract him to represent me. Because of more surgeries at the time, I didn't see this lawyer again until February 15th, 1988, when I informed him that I would like him to represent me in the lawsuit against the insurer. He accepted and told me that he would represent me personally, and his commission was now 50% whether the case was settled in court, or out of court. He would prepare a contingency fee form for us to sign.

On March 15th, 1988, I met Mr. Bukinshaw at his second office in Lost Hills, California. At this meeting, I told him that my primary physician, Dr. Cucumb, who rescued me in the canyon, had abused me sexually and had told me that by teaching me how to make love, it would help my brain to recover. Mr. Bukinshaw asked me how many people knew about this.

I explained that the psychiatrists, neuropsychiatrist, and psychologist who treated me knew about it, and they told me that this surgeon was using me and I should report him to the Medical Board of California.

After hearing my story, Mr. Bukinshaw asked me to talk to these doctors concerning a letter of diagnosis he would need for the insurer. He emphasized that I should tell the doctors not to speak about Dr. Cucumb and his sexual abuses. He wanted to use Dr. Cucumb as a major witness when we went to court.

"This is a five million dollar lawsuit, Mrs. Kuhlman," he said. "Tom Smith, another attorney with my firm, will work with me on your case."

We then signed a *Retainer Agreement* based on contingent fees, and he reminded me to tell my other doctors not to mention Dr. Cucumb's sexual abuses in their depositions and medical reports.

I came back home feeling powerless. Once again, I had to do exactly as instructed by my lawyer. I called at the offices of Drs. Krell, Andreassen, Futiles, and Lewin and made appointments. Dr. Andreassen, the first psychiatrist, who treated me in California after my comatose period, couldn't be reached. I saw these physicians the next week and told them that Mr. Bukinshaw did not want them to make any mention of Dr. Cucumb's sexual advances. My doctors told me, "If you don't report him, this neuro-surgeon will rape more patients. Odette Marie, what this doctor did to you wasn't correct. He raped you. He knew how injured you were."

Dr. Krell, a psychiatrist, offered to report Dr. Cucumb himself. "But the attorneys have forbidden me to talk to other people about that subject," I said. I really didn't know what to do. I had never heard of the California Medical Board before.

On October 12th, 1988, Mr. Bukinshaw called to inform me that our trial date had been postponed because the insurer had transferred the lawsuit from State Court to Federal Court. Furthermore, Mr. Bukinshaw informed me that he would go alone to Federal Court to get the case transferred back to the State Court. "The insurer is playing the game of transferring your lawsuit only to procrastinate and create problems," he said.

In December of 1988, Mr. Smith informed me that the insurer had again postponed the deposition until February, 1989. The same day, Joan, Mr. Bukinshaw's secretary, called to tell me that I needed a letter from each of my many doctors stating that I couldn't see them anymore because the insurer wouldn't cover the medical expenses.

At another meeting with Mr. Bukinshaw, where we discussed benefit forms, I noticed that no other lawyers were there working on my files. His secretary was gone, and his office was empty. I discussed Dr. Cucumb with him again, but he was adamant.

"You can't report Dr. Cucumb to the Medical Board. I'll need him if we go to court. When the case is settled, then you can report him. Let me do my job first."

At this point, my damaged brain didn't know what to think nor what to do. I didn't have any knowledge about the Medical Board, and I wasn't clear on just what should be done.

On April 4th, 1989, at seven in the morning, I went to Mr. Bukinshaw's office to prepare for my deposition. He wanted to be sure that I would not disclose the abuse by Dr. Cucumb to the defendant's lawyer. Also, he didn't want the defendant's lawyer to see my appointment book *(agenda)* that I had used as my second memory since my accident.

In September of 1989, when I was at Mr. Bukinshaw's office with his secretary to discuss a medical bill, I noticed a complex box of letters, files, and benefit statements relating to my case that had been torn apart. The secretary didn't know what happened. Later on, when my lawyer arrived at his office, I showed him the destroyed records.

"Don't worry," he said. "Joan and I are going to put everything back together. I apologize for what you found." I didn't fully understand and could only assume that he was responsible for the destruction of my documents.

On October 3rd, 1989, when I again met with Mr. Bukinshaw, he was very depressed. He said he was considering quitting the legal profession. He said that Mike, one of his employees, wasn't there that day to work on my case. "But, don't worry," he said. "I'll take care of it."

I asked about Tom Smith who was supposed to be working on the case with him, and was told for the first time that Mr. Smith wasn't working there any longer.

On October 11th, 1989, Mr. Bukinshaw called at my residence to tell me that he had lost the interrogatory papers and needed copies of the ones I had. When I met him in his office on October 23rd, he told me that the work on my case wasn't done and he didn't have a full-time secretary anymore.

"But the time limit to answer the insurer's questions was today, the 23rd," I said.

Mr. Bukinshaw grabbed the telephone and made a phone call to the defendant's lawyer, asking for one more extension.

He didn't have the interrogatories ready on October 30th either. Needless to say, I was upset.

"The defendant's attorney will never believe you're serious about the case because you don't answer their questions. And what about the depositions of Orange Health Insurance Company's employees?"

He told me they were not done.

"Now, you're telling me that nothing has been done. It's not a good sign. I don't want to lose my lawsuit because you aren't serious anymore."

"You won't lose. We have a good case."

"When I engaged you as my attorney, you told me that it was a very good case, worth 5 million dollars. Are you changing your mind?" I asked.

"What do you want me to say? I didn't do the work," he said.

"Don't say anything," I answered angrily, "Just do it. Do the work."

Mr. Bukinshaw told me that the work would be done Wednesday, November 1st.

On October 31st, he called to ask for the address of Coldwell Banker Residential Realtor, where I had practiced as a real estate agent, and also for the address of my former co-producer, Maria-Estela Lorca, from Buenos Aires, Argentina. Even though I gave him this information, he never contacted the real estate broker to establish my loss of income.

On March 13th, Mr. Bukinshaw called me to let me know that he felt positive about winning my case because of a meeting he had with the defense lawyer and the judge to discuss that my brain injury was a physical injury, and not a mental disorder. He asked for a letter outlining my recovery, which took over five years. He was going to Los Angeles Superior Court with the defendant's lawyer on March 27th to obtain a judgment.

The next day, he told me that he believed we would get a maximum of 500,000 dollars from the insurer for negligence because the Judge, Iain McCormick, declared that brain damage was a physical injury.

I received a medical report in the mail written by Dr. Cucumb that was in error. The report stated that his care stopped in October of 1985 when, in fact, in May of 1986, he had performed the pseudarthrosis on my back with Dr. Maker. I called Mr. Bukinshaw to inform him of the mistake.

"I want you to be at my office on Monday, April 23rd. I'll call Dr. Cucumb when you are here," he said.

When I arrived at Mr. Bukinshaw's office, after having postponed the appointment until the next day, he asked for Dr. Cucumb's phone number.

"I'll call him after you leave," Mr. Bukinshaw said. "I don't want you to talk to anyone about Dr. Cucumb's sexual abuses."

His behavior puzzled me. In June, I wrote to him again concerning unpaid medical bills. He advised me not to appear in court because the insurer had made an offer. He said that on the 9th of July, he would go to court with two other attorneys to present our case to a judge.

"Don't worry. We're all prepared. I'll call you when I come back from court."

On July 9th, Mr. Bukinshaw called me before going to court for arbitration of assignment of a trial date.

"What about the emotional suffering that the insurer caused me and the fact that I was raped by Dr. Cucumb because I was seriously injured and unable to defend myself?"

"I'll call you when I come back from court and we'll talk about that,"Mr. Bukinshaw answered.

At two fifty eight in the afternoon, I called my attorney and he told me that the judge decided to continue the discovery period to September 7th. If we went to court, it would be within four months, and Dr. Cucumb would be our best witness.

In July, I met again with Mr. Bukinshaw in his office after he called and said it was important that I meet with him. When I sat down, the first thing he said was, "I'm broke. I'm considering getting Mr. Ken Genfasst, an attorney who specializes in this type of lawsuit, to work with me. It won't cost you anything. I would share my commission with him."

I listened to what he had to say, not knowing what to think. He put three white forms on his desk in front of me and said, "Sign here . . . here . . . and here. I won't use them before you read it." In addition, he told me, "I want you to loan me between twenty thousand and thirty thousand dollars for my expenses."

"I don't have any money."

"Can Mr. Fischer pay for you? Or can your daughter pay?" he asked.

"No. My daughter is only fifteen years old. She has been supporting me since the day of the accident. And David has nothing to do with this lawsuit."

I left his office very upset. I couldn't understand the game he was playing. Inside, I knew something was very wrong. That night, I didn't sleep at all. I kept thinking about the white forms he had me sign. My brain was still living in the past, hearing my mother tell me when I was young never to sign a blank piece of paper.

The next morning, I drove to his office and said I was there to pick up the three forms I'd signed before. I told him I felt uncomfortable about them.

"You could have called me concerning the verification forms instead of coming here," Mr. Bukinshaw said.

"I was going to Cedars-Sinai Medical Center, so on my way, I stopped here," I said. He gave me the forms but I never found out what he wanted to do with these signed forms. I was just uncomfortable and afraid.

On August 7th, 1990, Mr. Bukinshaw called to inform me that the insurer had made an offer of 50,000 dollars. He postponed my exam with their neurologist in West Los Angeles.

Later, he called again to say he needed to see both David and me together. I asked him if he had contacted Ken Genfasst regarding my lawsuit.

"Odette Marie, I didn't contact him because I'd lose control of your case if I deal with him. I worked very hard on this lawsuit. I just need to see you and David."

"There is no reason for David and I to see you . . . if you have been unable to make an appointment with Mr. Genfasst," I said.

"I had an appointment with Ken in the past, but he didn't show up. I don't like people that act that way." This response upset me.

"Mr. Bukinshaw, if you are afraid to lose control of the lawsuit, this is only your ego."

"Odette Marie," he said, "let me talk to David. I want an appointment with both of you. He's going to benefit from this money. He should be the first one to be contacted. I need between twenty and thirty thousand dollars. I have to take some depositions. If you had given me this lawsuit the first time that I saw you in 1986, we would have been finished with it, and you would have received over 5 million dollars."

"Mr. Bukinshaw, we are wasting our time. Neither David nor my fifteen-year-old daughter have the money you want. This lawsuit is between Orange Health Insurance Company, you, and I. You are not going to get any money out of my daughter or David. They don't have it to give you," I replied.

"The next time that David comes here with you to talk to me and sits in my office, I'll charge him," Bukinshaw said.

"Why don't you just call Ken, the other attorney you were talking about? I would like to talk with him. You told me in the past that this lawyer could take my case on contingency. I believe that we need a more experienced attorney with the tools to win this lawsuit, someone who is professional and not afraid to work honestly."

"Odette Marie, I know another lawyer that is very good in bad faith cases. I'll call him. I'd prefer it anyway. I have to go now, I have work to do. Don't worry. I like you, you're very nice, everything will be fine."

He then made an appointment for me on Tuesday morning at eight o'clock. He said he needed to see me before the insurer's lawyer and he took Dr. Cucumb's deposition, which had been postponed to August 29 per his request.

Later in August, Mr. Bukinshaw showed me a letter from the insurer which talked about my previous attorney, Mr. Anson, and his claim that the mental health dollar amount limit should not apply in my case because of my accident. Cost containment on mental health expenditures was a popular issue with insurers, but they were worried that if they could not prove that I had prior mental illness, they might lose the case. "Prior to your accident, were you ever paranoid or schizophrenic?" Mr. Bukinshaw asked me.

"I've never heard these words," I said.

"Fine, let me give you the names of the lawyers that I've chosen to work with me." He gave me a piece of yellow paper on which to write. Then he said, "I won't lose control of your case with these lawyers. Regis O'Looney is one young lawyer that will probably be working on the case. It isn't decided for sure yet."

I was confused by all the changing of attorneys, but decided to go along with Mr. Bukinshaw. I asked how the depositions were going.

"Your psychiatrist, Dr. Krell, was impeccable, very professional during his deposition," he said.

On September 13th, 1990, Mr. Bukinshaw, who had just returned from a vacation in New York, called me sounding very positive about our lawsuit. He informed me that the new attorneys in Los Angeles were now working with him. They took the depositions of

Dr. Deavila, psychologist, and Dr. Lewin, neuropsychiatrist. Mr. Bukinshaw told me that they described me as *"cognizant,"* although I was not sure what he meant. On September 17th, he wanted me to meet with the Los Angeles lawyers. I told him that I wanted David to come too. He said he would meet us at the Los Angeles office.

At the meeting, the lawyer sounded very optimistic. Mr. Greg White, Mr. Bukinshaw and I signed an agreement, agreeing to send me a copy in the mail. During our meeting, I told the new lawyers, White and O'Looney, that I had been sexually abused by Dr. Cucumb after I came out of the coma, and that if I had not had a brain injury, it would not have happened.

I also had been informed by my neurologist that it was now too late to relearn by therapy. The treatment has to be given immediately after the brain damage, not years later. Therefore, the only way that I had to relearn was with the help of my daughter and by myself. I didn't have the financial means to hire a tutor and my insurer had refused to pay for any treatments.

I filed a lawsuit for punitive damages/bad faith against Orange Health Insurance Company, but for the time being, having a lawsuit against the insurer didn't bring me any cash, and didn' t make the insurer see their bad faith actions against their client. Only time would tell. When the case goes to trial, the Judge might force the insurer to cover all medical expenses, plus force them to pay for having made me wait months and years to receive the proper medical treatment and therapy.

CHAPTER 17 - MARRIAGE
Taking Charge

On December 29th, 1988, Véronique and I had a meeting with Mr. Ronald Brook, an attorney from Mr. Gaines' office. I asked if January 30th, 1989, would be the last day to go to court for the case against the State of California.

"You should know that a Judge always has the power to postpone your lawsuit for another five years if he wants to," Mr. Brook answered.

We were shocked! Véronique said, "Mother, David may die before our lawsuit is over, and I'll never have a daddy."

"Sweetheart, don't cry, Mother will take care of this problem. You'll have a daddy. I promise you that." We left the law office at three thirty in the afternoon, and Véronique asked if she could invite her friend, Lisa, to sleep over. There was already a message at home from Lisa inviting my daughter to her house to spend the night.

The next morning, I began my six-mile walk, talking over the situation with my father in my mind, telling him how Véronique and I felt about being captives of the legal system. Six years and three days had passed since John died and Véronique had lost her father. With every step I took, I would pray for guidance. On the last two miles of my walk, I felt that I could hear my father telling me to get remarried. A joy ran through my body as I knew this was my father's voice talking to me and telling me the right thing to do. In my heart, the only person that could stop me from getting remarried was David, by refusing.

When I came home, the first thing I did was to wake David.

"David wake up, I'm ready to marry you," I said.

He turned in the bed with his eyes closed while I shook his shoulder. "Darling, I accept. I'll marry you tomorrow." Still rubbing sleep from his eyes, he sat up in the bed. "Are you sure? I've already asked you twice and you always refused because of your lawsuits."

"Don't worry, I'm prepared to marry you tomorrow," I said. "But what about your lawsuit against the State of California? Your lawyer wants you to be a widow when you go to court."

"Sweetheart, you're worth more than $23 million I don't care about the lawyers and their millions. I talked with father this morning when I was walking, and he told me to get remarried. So, if you're ready, I am too."

That day, David called Caesar's Palace in Las Vegas to make reservations for a suite for us and a bedroom for Véronique. When I called her, she became very excited.

"Mother, can I tell Lisa about it?"

"Yes, you can tell Lisa. And tell her that her mother hopes she will accept an invitation to come too, to be another witness."

I heard squeals of laughter from the girls. "Now both of you come home as soon as possible. We're leaving in two hours and need to get prepared."

I had decided in my heart and mind that no more lawyers would stop us from rebuilding our lives. Life was too short. If you find

July 24, 1971, the beautiful day it was for John and I. Our marriage ceremony took place in Québec City. Old fashioned horses and carriages were our way of transportation.

Arriving at 'Studio de Dance Roland Hallé' where the reception took place. From left to right my father-in-law, Bud Kuhlman, Claude Ruel, Johé Poulin, John and me with my niece Caroline Pouliot, our flower girl.

The international family I have now. From left to right, my mom, Juliette, my dad, Léopold, myself, John, Lenore, Bud and Caroline.

My loving husband John tastes our wedding cake.

John and I with our champagne of international love,
Canada and United States of America.

The love that we shared.

Snow shoes (racket) for a wedding gift? From left to right, John's sister, Lynn, my dad, Léopold, John, his brother, Corky and a family friend, Marie-Paul Poulin.

Reverend Richard Andrews, me and David

Beauty of Love

happiness, you must take it. Don't let it go.

On the drive to Las Vegas, David turned to me and said, "What are you going to say to your attorneys?"

"No one should worry about the legal system and these lawyers." I smiled at my daughter. "Véronique, your mother is getting remarried for sure. I'm doing what Grandpapa Bourget advised me to do. As for the lawyers, I'll write and send them a copy of my marriage certificate."

In my mind, I decided that the wedding should be entirely for David, Véronique and I. I was not going to think about guests. That wasn't important in my second life. Time is precious, and I wanted to share it only in the ways I wished, and not worry about anybody else.

I remembered July 24th, 1971, the date of my extravagant first marriage. At that time, I was a business woman and public figure in the media. Physical beauty was very important. We were driven to the ceremony in an old fashioned horse and carriage. Everything was perfectly planned. At that time of my life, I had an administrator in charge of organizing everything. Since I had been reborn, my vision of what was important had changed.

So, on December 31st, 1988, with Lisa acting as David's witness, and Véronique as mine, we were married in our suite at Ceasar's Palace. David's family and my family didn't know anything about the event.

After the marriage ceremony was over, I called my mother in Québec City to tell her the news. She was extremely happy for all of us, but surprised that no family was invited. We returned to Los Angeles after the New Year to get on with our lives.

At my next appointment with Mr. Bukinshaw I told him that I had gotten remarried on December 31st.

"Did you marry Mr. Fischer?" he asked.

"Yes, I married David. We're very happy together, and my daughter now has a daddy."

"I would have preferred that you waited until the lawsuit was over," he said. I didn't care. I also wrote a letter to Mr. Gaines announcing the marriage and enclosed a copy of the certificate. I didn't receive any congratulations card or letter back. But it was fine with me. After six years as a widow, in my mind I felt that the lawyers should do their job as lawyers, and let me live my life with my daughter and my new husband.

IN CHARGE

Since my marriage, I no longer needed to be insured by my old company, Orange Health and Casualty Insurance. I was finally independent. After waiting six months, I'd be able to get medical treatment that would be paid by David' health insurer. I was still experiencing pain in my back, neck and shoulder. I didn't want to continue taking pain medication forever.

After visiting several clinics, I joined the therapy clinic at Los Robles Medical Center. Catherine, a physical therapy technician, kept telling me, "Odette Marie, your neck is so tight. We really have to work on getting it to relax."

She continually worked on that section of my neck and said she could feel that something was not correct. After two and a half months, while she was massaging my neck, she told me she felt a nerve release.

"I don't know what you just touched, but I felt great pain, like something came loose," I said.

"Move your head to the right and then to the left, please," Catherine said. I did as she said and the pain was gone. My head no longer felt too heavy for my neck.

"What did you do? The pain is gone."

"You probably had a nerve impingement and now it's been released. That's why you feel no pain. But there are no guarantees, it could get displaced again."

"At any time?"

"Yes, but don't panic. We know what it is now and we can always manipulate it." Seven months have passed since that day and I no longer have the neck pain. Dr. Phillip also prescribed a new type of orthopedic pillow, which helped.

I had three months of physical treatment on my right shoulder. An **MRI** showed nothing wrong. My physicians explained that tests would not necessarily show all problems, especially if tissue was injured. They tried cortisone, but it didn't help. I began exercising my arm intensely every morning.

On October 3rd, 1990, surgery was done on my right shoulder at Cedars-Sinai Medical Center on an outpatient basis. During the evening, the surgeon called me at home to see how I was and to inform me not to lie down on my right shoulder. Following the surgery, I started exercising my arm and my shoulder every morning for twenty times. I repeated this exercise at night ten more times. I didn't have any pain and knew that the physical injuries were fixed, even though the pre-surgery tests showed nothing wrong.

On November 2nd, 1990, I met the surgeon at his office for a follow up.

"Would you look at me, Dr. Phillip?" I said. "I can move my arm up and down now without any difficulty. What do you think of that?" I was so exhilarated to be free of pain. The last physical problem had been eliminated. I was able to sleep on my right side for the first time in seven years.

This was one more victory on my road to recovery. I share my physical injuries with you because I would like you to understand that you're the only one who knows your own body. Always take time to listen and study it. You're the only one who can tell if something is wrong. Trust yourself. It could help you understand your own physical and emotional pain more clearly.

CHAPTER 18 - JUDGMENT

One Monday morning, at eight o'clock, Mary Symthe, the secretary from Mr. Anson's office, called to inform me that he had been appointed Superior Court Judge in San Francisco. His law firm sent cards to all his clients confirming this prestigious news. I was surprised they let me know since I had retained another attorney.

On January 30th, 1989, David and I drove to Superior Court in Los Angeles again, but Mr. Gaines wasn't there. Another of his young lawyer associates was in court to represent me. The trial was postponed. I became upset and said to the young attorney, "I was raped by my primary physician and Mr. Gaines doesn't want me to report him to the Medical Board of California because he'll need him when the case goes to trial. You can tell your boss . . . I have had enough. My psychiatrists want me to report this doctor." The only thing the young attorney was able to say was, "The trial was postponed."

On March 6th, 1989, we went back to court and Mr. Gaines was absent. Another associate, Mr. Nordick, was present to represent me. As usual, the trial was postponed until September 29th.

On April 10th, 1989, a young lawyer from Mr. Gaines' office

called me from the courthouse to ask the name of the medical doctor that rescued me in the mountains. He told me that the jury would be chosen tomorrow, and the following day I should be in court. It was the beginning of the trial.

"How can the trial of my case start tomorrow when I haven't been prepared? Mr. Gaines didn't inform me of anything regarding the process of the trial. What's happening?" I asked.

The young attorney didn't know the answer. He repeated, "The trial starts tomorrow. If Mr. Gaines didn't prepare you, it's too bad because you must be there tomorrow."

In court the next day, Mr. Gaines showed up. David, Lisette, a friend, and I were nervous. My attorney took me aside in a corner in the corridor and said, "We can choose a jury, but it would be better if we refuse because three other cases like yours were in court this year with a jury and they all lost."

"What do you advise me to do?" I asked.

"It's better for us if we go with the judge."

I accepted his advice. Mr. Gaines also told me, "It's better if the jury or the judge see you without your new husband. Ask David not to stay near you."

I walked over to my husband and repeated what the lawyer had said regarding his presence in court, and David left the courthouse for the balance of the day. I felt very insecure without him there.

Lisette and I entered the courtroom for the start of the trial.They called me to the witness stand and swore me in. Then the defense attorney started to ask me questions. I was very nervous. I remembered nothing about the accident. My body was severely injured, but how it happened, I didn't know. I knew only what the newspaper and other people told me. It was terrible. At the end of the day, my lawyer told me to be back in court the day after at ten thirty in the morning with my daughter. She would take the stand after lunch, around one thirty PM.

"Ask David to bring Véronique to court tomorrow," Mr. Gaines said.

We returned again the next day, and after lunch Véronique was sworn in. My daughter was only seven years old when the accident happened. Now, eight years later, the legal system was asking a child to remember what happened. What caused the accident? How did your daddy die?

On other days, more witnesses (Sheriff deputy, parents of other victims) took the stand. Every witness I met in court asked about my daughter and told me how terrifying it was to see the canyon area where the accident happened. I also met the other survivor; a young man who had fallen two hundred and ten feet. I was so happy to meet him. He was, without any doubt, the only person who knew what I was going through. We had fallen in the same area during the same week.

One Sheriff told me how he appreciated having my daughter at the scene of the accident. "Without her," he said, "We wouldn't have been able to rescue you alive. She directed us to where you were."

On Friday, April 14th, 1989, we left the courthouse after the judge informed us that we should be back on Monday, April 17th, at ten thirty in the morning. He would give us his verdict then. David, Lisette and I returned once more to the Los Angeles Superior Court on that day to find out if I had won or lost this lawsuit.

To my surprise, the judge arrived on the bench to inform us that he had reached a tentative verdict for a period of ten days in favor of the State of California. But, he retained the power to change his mind at any time. He asked the defense attorney to prepare the Statement of Decision. My lawyer asked to have the defense send him a copy of the Statement of Decision. The judge agreed to his request.

We all left the courtroom together, David, Lisette, Mr. Gaines and myself. Mr. Gaines told me, "I'll call your previous attorney, Mr. Anson, and see what we can do. I'll let you know what happens."

"What about the miniature mountain that Mr. Anson had made to present in court?" I asked.

"I showed it to the judge in his chambers," he said.
That was it. Mr. Gaines left the courtroom. My husband, my girlfriend and I stayed there a little bit longer to talk.

"I'm glad it's finally over. The lawyers were trying this case only for money, and they lost. I've finally got my freedom," I said.

David was very discouraged. I went on, "Nobody knows when they're born and nobody knows when it is their time to die. I feel that this is the only justice in life."

"Odette Marie, do you realize you probably lost your case?" David said.

"Yes, I know, but I don't care. I was never a millionaire before, therefore, I didn't lose anything. Darling, I lost my health in this accident, and this million couldn't buy back my health, and couldn't buy our love. I'm alive, and I've relearned how to walk. I'm relearning every day with you and Véronique. What more can you want in life, sweetheart?

David looked at me sadly. Lisette patted my hand.

"Try to realize that I won. Because I was almost dead and today I'm here, married to you, and I can raise my daughter. I never lost this $23 million since I never had it. Try to accept me the way I am."

"Honey, you've suffered for eight years. You lost everything you had; your husband, your health, your intellectual capacity. Your daughter was injured emotionally. You've been paying a fortune for medical care, all this because of the negligence of an employee of the State. That, I can't take. Don't they owe you something for that?" David asked.

On the way home, David suggested we stop at Mr. Bukinshaw's office, the insurance lawsuit attorney, and ask him his opinion about this judge. We stopped and called, and Mr. Bukinshaw agreed to see us.

An hour later, we arrived at his office and explained what happened when we were in court. We told him that we got a tentative verdict for ten days in favor of the State of California.

"What's the name of the judge?" he asked. I gave him my notebook *(agenda)* and said, "Here it is. This is his name. Can you read it?"

"I know this judge. He's an idiot. Your lawyer should appeal."

"How do you know him?" I asked.

"I met him in a lawsuit when he was an attorney," Mr. Bukinshaw said. He's really an idiot," he repeated.

I called Mr. Gaines' office to see if we had grounds to appeal the case, but he wasn't there. Later, a young associate called and told me that Mr. Gaines would call me if we lost the case. On May 15th, the day of the final decision, I never received a phone call nor letter from Mr. Gaines.

I spoke to a friend of the family, John, who was also an attorney and asked if he could come to the Los Angeles Courthouse to look over the results of my case. Over a month passed and I still had not been notified. Did I win or did I lose? John and I arrived at the courthouse, went to the filing department and asked a clerk to see the file for case number C-059-834. After looking, the clerk came back to the counter and informed us that the judge had every-thing relating to the case in his chamber in Department E. John and I left more confused than when we came in.

"This doesn't make any sense," I said. "The judge told us that in ten days he was going to let us know his final verdict. That was a month ago. Why do you think it is taking so long?"

But, John was also in the dark.

I came back home exhausted and explained the situation to my husband.

"I told you sweetheart, don't waste your time. The judge will let you know only when he is ready. Just don't worry about it," David said.

Even as my husband and daughter told me not to worry, I couldn't help being upset at the legal system. How could they stall citizens off so long, hanging by a cord for months, years, before going to court? And why, after a week in the court, did the judge say he wasn't sure who was responsible, that he needed ten more days to think about it? What kind of a game is that? Is it another ego power trip?

On May 30th, 1989, I called Mr. Gaines to obtain the list of medical doctors who had a lien against my case, but no one was available to help me. Inside, I thought that if I lost the case, I was sure Mr. Gaines would inform the doctors. I also wanted to find out if I lost or won.

By June 1st, I still had no news. When I called Mr. Gaines' office to let him know that I would be out of town June 4th through June 11th, his secretary answered, "Mr. Gaines will call you when there is something," she said.

On June 13th, I called Mr. Gaines' office twice to get the list of doctors who had liens against my case. The secretary informed me that it would take too long to get the list since she didn't have the files. After she said she knew nothing about the decision on the case, I asked again to speak to Mr. Gaines.

"Mrs. Kuhlman," she said "You shouldn't worry about the case. You should only take care of the liens because Mr. Gaines is taking care of the lawsuit."

On June 14th, I called Los Angeles Superior Court and asked the Clerk if the Judge had given his final verdict, but she told me I had to be there in person to find out. She couldn't tell me anything concerning my lawsuit on the telephone.

I called Mr. Gaines again on July 8th and July 24th and asked to speak to another attorney, when Mr. Gaines would not return my calls. He never did call me back. On July 25th, David and I went to the court and got a copy of the Statement of Decision, plus a copy of the Judgment. This is where we learned for the first time that I had lost my lawsuit. My attorney, Mr. Gaines, had known about the Judgment since May 17th, 1989, but never informed us. I paid to have copies of these papers made .

On July 26th, I again called Mr. Gaines, but couldn't get past his secretary. She said she would have a Mr. Nordick call back, but he never did. On July 27th, I sent registered letters to them. Finally, on August 4th, I received a letter telling me to remember that I had only sixty days from the date of Notice of Entry of Judgment to file for an appeal. It was too late. The sixty days had passed. I received the letter eighty days after the date of Notice of Entry of Judgment.

I called Mr. Gaines, but he refused to take my phone call. I had lost my rights as a citizen to appeal my case because of my own attorney's incompetent and unprofessional behavior. I supposed his ego couldn't accept having lost the suit. It's hard to believe that this is the way the legal system functions in the State of California.

With one problem after another. I still had one more pending legal burden, my suit against my insurer. In September, Mr. Bukinshaw called to inform me that Dr. Cucumb's deposition had been postponed again. The law firm was to answer questions of the insurer on September 28th, 1990. I was scheduled to have a medical examination by the insurer's physicians. They took an ***electro-encephalogram***, another type of brain test, and ***MRI, (cervical, lumbar)*** and ***brain stem test***.

In October, I called Mr. Bukinshaw and the other law firm to ask what the results of my medical tests revealed. None of the attorneys working on my case were available, so I was transferred to a law clerk. When I asked more questions about getting copies of the depositions of my own physicians, particularly Dr. Cucumb's, I was told that it took several weeks for the depositions to be written up and available for distribution. The clerk also informed me that he didn't have any information available about the results of my tests. None of these attorneys would return my phone calls, even though I left messages.

Finally, on December 4th, 1990, Mr. Bukinshaw called and asked if I had received copies of the depositions. He reminded me that I should not report Dr. Cucumb's sexual conduct to the State Medical Board, after telling me that Mr. O'Looney had the depositions.

When I didn't receive copies of the depositions by December 17th, I called Mr. O'Looney to inquire about them. The receptionist said that he wasn't there, but he would call me back. O'Looney never returned my phone call, nor did any of the other attorneys in the firm. None of them wanted to talk to me about depositions. My psychiatrists and neurophychiatrist still wanted Dr. Cucumb to be reported to the Medical Board of California.

Mr. Bukinshaw and the other attorneys were supposed to exchange expert witness information before January 7th, 1991. When I called to find out if this had been done, Mr. Bukinshaw said they had forgotten about it, but not to worry. He would find a way to handle it. I was later told that these depositions had to be postponed. Mr. Bukinshaw also told me that he and his partners were considering a **"Rent-A-Judge"** to settle the lawsuit out of court. I was totally confused, not understanding what was going on and I communicated this to my attorney. I didn't have any idea what he was doing with my case.

"Odette Marie," Mr. Bukinshaw said, "Don't worry. One of our attorneys, Mr. Greg White, is a good friend of Judge Kevin Hall. I'll tell you more about it when the case is settled. I can't talk about it now."

On January 21st, 1991, a pre-deposition conference between Mr. O'Looney and Judge Hall was suppose to take place. The next day, I drove to the defense attorney's office in Los Angeles for the completion of my deposition. After stating my name for the record, the defendant's lawyer asked me if I recalled having done this before. To refresh my memory, he discussed a few things about the procedure. Then, he told me to speak slowly because I had a French accent. He reminded me that if I didn't understand the questions, to take my time and think it out. I had to try to give as good and complete answer as I could. The attorney explained that I would have a chance later on to review the transcript of the deposition, and be allowed to make changes in it, or delete things from it.

Then he asked my lawyer questions about my wage loss documents; one from Maria-Estela Lorca, producer, and one from

Coldwell Banker Residential Real Estate showing a commission breakdown. Mr. O'Looney had nothing to show even though I had given his partner, Mr. Bukinshaw, these data in writing.

The defense attorney asked me questions regarding my work and income before the accident. I answered the best I could, but I wasn't allowed to look in my notebook *(agenda)* or my papers to give complete answers. My primary lawyer, Mr. Bukinshaw, had answers to all these questions. Mr. O'Looney said he would look for the information and give copies to the defense attorney. In front of everyone there, I said to O'Looney,

"Please, don't forget to present these wage loss documents."

"I won't," he answered.

The deposition continued regarding the names of many medical care providers that had refused to treat me because the insurer refused to cover the medical expenses. The defense attorney wanted to know what I was treated for, when I was hospitalized, dates of treatment, the names of persons who were in the emergency room, etc. I could have answered some of their questions if I had been permitted to look at my notebook. But, with brain damage and a period of blankness during my coma, it was impossible for me to remember all of these data by heart.

The defense attorney asked what an employee at the emergency hospital had said to my driver. I was unable to recall the conversation between my drivers, John and Arlene and the emergency hospital employee. We were talking about a period of 9 years since some of the events had taken place, and they were expecting me to remember everything by heart. I was very upset.

Later on during the day, the defense attorney asked my lawyer for the dollar amount that we were claiming in this action for general damages. My lawyers had not determined an amount at that time. Then they wanted to know if we had determined an amount for punitive damages. The only thing my lawyer was able to tell him was that we had not determined an exact amount, but expected it to be more than $2 million. When asked what this amount was based on, O'Looney said it was for general damages, suffering, pain, aggravation and the ability to be retrained.

I was then asked the type of drugs the neuropsychiatrist, Dr. Lewin, had prescribed for me when I was his patient many years ago. I answered as best I could. The defense attorney finally referred to Dr. Andreassen's records which disclosed that I apparently had had a sexual relationship with Dr. Cucumb. He asked me if this was correct.

I knew that I had never had a consensual sexual relationship with my primary physician and I said, "How do you call that?" I could not understand the terms he used. The defense attorney wanted to know if I understood the question . . . and my lawyer also asked me if I understood the question. I understood what they were saying, but was unable to recall the correct term because of my limited memory. The defense attorney searched for more information from Dr. Andreassen and went on.

He read to me from the psychiatrist's (Dr. Andreassen) report and I recalled the following. Before John died, I lived alone with my daughter for three years. I had no sex at all, but after my accident, this doctor used me sexually. I could recall nothing about my comatose period or immediately afterward. Then, in notes from the psychiatrist's data, it said that on June 12th, 1984, Dr. Andreassen asked me if Dr. Cucumb was in his 40s. I stated that I thought he might be 40 years of age. The defense attorney told me about the entry of October 21st, 1984. It stated that Dr. Cucumb had kept me alive, and that I had a debt to him and it had to be paid with sex.

The defense attorney asked again if I had a sexual relationship with Dr. Cucumb. My answer was, "Yes, but not . . ." Before I could explain, my attorney, Mr. O'Looney, looked at me with a terrible expression on his face and said, "You've just answered the question."

Inside of me, I felt that I had not answered the question. They would not let me explain and I had difficulty describing what had happened. I never had a consensual sexual relationship with Dr. Cucumb or any other physician. I had been taken advantage of at a time when I was vulnerable. Their questions made me feel like crying. The defense attorney continued, asking me again if my answer was yes. Very aggressively I answered, "I got raped." He then wanted to know over what period of time I had this relation-ship. My lawyer objected, asking the purpose of these questions. The other attorney stated that it was a critical issue. My lawyer, O'Looney, wanted this conversation about sexual abuses to stop, but the defense attorney insisted on continuing.

I was asked if Dr. Cucumb ever told me about the possible ill effects of his having a sexual relationship with me as his patient. I asked the lawyer if he could repeat that slowly so that my brain could register what he wanted. He restated his question differently and informed me that the State of California Board of Medical Quality Assurance watches over behavior of this sort, incidents of sexual relationship between medical doctors and their patients. Again he asked me if Dr. Cucumb had discussed with me the possible ill effect on my health, especially my mental health, of him having a sexual relationship with me.

I looked at the defendant's lawyer, and I said, "Okay, what he told me . . ." Then I stopped and asked O'Looney, "Can I tell him what he said?"

O'Looney answered angrily, "No. Just answer the question."

At that time of my life, my brain didn't have the capacity to just answer the question. I wasn't even sure if what they said was a question or not. It irritated me to see that my own lawyer wanted to hide the truth . . . the facts. I went on telling the defense attorney that Dr. Cucumb said I had brain damage in the accident. When he came to my house and I answered the door, I didn't know who he was or anything.

The defense attorney asked if I was talking about my residence.

"Yes," I answered. "He came to my house, and he said that I wasn't allowed to be up because I was too injured, that I should be in bed."

My lawyer said, "I believe that she has answered the question."

But, the defense attorney wanted to know more about the fact that it wasn't a consensual sexual relationship, that I was raped. He asked what I meant by that. I explained that Dr. Cucumb had told me after my brain injury that I was a person with a high libido. The defense attorney asked me to repeat my answer. I explained again what Dr. Cucumb had told me; "Since your brain injury, you're a high libido person, and I must teach you how to make love, otherwise your brain will never be normal because you have brain damage."

"Dr. Cucumb told you that?" The defense attorney asked. "Did you believe him?" "I don't know." I cried. "I was mentally and physically not there at that time. Anybody could have said any-thing they wanted. I was too ill to really understand what he was talking about."

My lawyer was very upset because I wanted to tell the truth. He looked at me and said, "You've answered the question."

But the defense attorney had more to say. He wanted to explain what these questions had to do with the charges and the seriousness of my condition. He believed that Dr. Cucumb's behavior compounded my progress, that I didn't receive enough psychiatric care. My progress, mental, psychiatric, and psychological, was impeded because of this behavior.

My lawyer and I sat listening while the defense attorney talked about Dr. Cucumb. Even though I had difficulty understanding much of his language, I thought that my lawyer was there to disclose the facts entirely. The conversation continued between the two lawyers. At one point, my lawyer decided that he would let the defense attorney go on only up to a certain point. The defense lawyer didn't like that limit. He told my lawyer that he better let him go on or he was going to take all of us downtown. (I assumed that the defense attorney met that he would take us to the District Attorney if my lawyer tried to stop him.)

Then he continued asking me questions about Dr. Cucumb. He asked how long the relationship went on with Dr. Cucumb. I explained how Dr. Cucumb had acted.

"He called and said that he was calling from his car. His car was parked at my front door."

Apparently, I wasn't answering his question correctly. Very angrily, my lawyer looked at me and said, "For how long a period of time is what he's asking."

The defense attorney very politely told me that he wanted to know if Dr. Cucumb came to my home for a number of weeks or months. He just wanted to know the truth.

I was under a lot of pressure after the long period of questioning. I finally understood what he was asking me and told both lawyers that Dr. Cucumb abused me sexually until my first back surgery was done in November, 1983. I still did not understand if the defense attorney was talking about the times that Dr. Cucumb came to my residence or the incidents that took place at his office and in the hospital. He then asked if Dr. Cucumb had treated me right after my accident. All I knew was that Dr. Cucumb told me he came to the canyon to rescue me.

During this time of questioning, I felt very nervous and exhausted. I was shocked by the fact that the defendant's lawyer knew so much about Dr. Cucumb's abuse when my own attorneys had forbidden me to report him to the Medical Board of California, and had forbidden me to talk to the defense attorney about it. I felt lost and couldn't understand the game Mr. Bukinshaw and his new partners were playing.

It was unbelievable to see Mr. O'Looney's behavior. No one had ever told me that the defense attorneys had been told of the sexual abuse. Mr. Bukinshaw didn't want me to be honest with my feelings, advising me not to report Dr. Cucumb to the Medical Board of California, like my psychiatrists had told me to.

Bukinshaw's new partner, Mr. O'Looney, just took over. When I asked to see a copy of my own deposition, he said, "I'm working on the case. You don't need a copy of your deposition. You do just what I want you to do." I thought I was entitled to a copy like the defense attorneys had explained at the beginning of my depositions.

When I reported to the courthouse in Santa Barbara County on February 6th, 1992, for the Pretrial Voluntary Conference, Mr. Bukinshaw had already explained that they had retained Judge Kevin Hall under the **"Rent-A-Judge"** program. At the courthouse, I asked Mr. O'Looney who was representing me to introduce me to the judge.

duce me to the judge.

"No. I don't want you to see the judge," he said.

"I insist," I said.

"You're not going to see him," O'Looney said. "I don't want you to. You do what I say."

I opened my purse and took out a small recording machine, asking if he would record the proceedings. O'Looney refused again.

I waited for a long time until O'Looney came out and told me they were discussing a settlement of $100,000. This made me angry. Had my attorneys even said anything about the fact that I was handicapped for the balance of my life? A large part of that was caused by the negligence of my health insurer. I wasn't even allowed to talk to the judge or the defense attorney about my physical injuries that were now permanent. Or about the fact that I had been sexually abused, and the insurer wouldn't pay for psychiatric care.

"I won't accept that amount of money," I told O'Looney. Mr. Bukinshaw always told me that this lawsuit was worth over $5 million. Last week, during my deposition, you told the defendant's lawyer that you were talking over $2 million. What kind of game are you playing? I want to call Mr. Bukinshaw. I need to speak to him."

Mr. O'Looney took me to a conference room and I called my first lawyer, explaining what had occurred.

"Odette Marie, I advise you to accept this offer. Otherwise, you'll ruin everything." Mr. Bukinshaw told me.

Why was no one able to be honest with me, even my own attorneys? I felt these lawyers were abusing me mentally, one after the other. They acted like a bunch of crooks and I didn't know why.

O'Looney went back to see the judge and the defense attorney.

After a while, he came out and said, "That figure is what they are offering you." I felt terrible and didn't know what to do. I had waited a long time, a total of nine years, to get the proper treatment because my insurer would not honor our contract. I felt my own attorneys had not presented information about my severe and permanent injuries, and the tremendous physical and emotional pain I had suffered when doctors refused treatment. The small amount the insurer offered would not even cover all of my medical expenses.

Then, Mr. O'Looney told me, "If you don't accept this amount, you'll have to give me 30,000 dollars to continue work on your case."

I could not understand what had happened. Why was my own attorney acting this way? What happened to the 5 million dollars and 2 million dollars figures?

O'Looney made me sign a form accepting the offer. Because he was so forceful, he gave me no choice.

The next day, I called Mr. Bukinshaw to discuss his 50% commission, stating that there would be nothing left to pay my doctors' bills.

"Don't pay any of them," he said. "It's been over 4 years, and they haven't sued you. Therefore, you don't owe them anything."

I couldn't believe it. These lawyers were nothing but a bunch of crooks. I was stunned and so affected by their behavior, that I went for a return meeting with my psychiatrist to discuss what had happened.

On February 4th, Mr. O'Looney called to tell me to come to his office to get the check from Orange Health Insurance Company. I asked for an earlier appointment, but he refused. When I arrived, he was standing with the check in his hand, talking at a speed that my brain couldn't register or make sense of. He put some papers in front of me and told me to sign them. I said that I wanted to read the papers before signing, but he refused.

"It will take too long," he said, "and I'm tired. If you don't sign, I can't give you your check. I'll have to return it to Orange Health Insurance."

I told him that I would sign but I wanted to know what it was about. He denied my request and refused to explain what the papers meant.

"Sign here beside each name," he said. I felt I had no choice but to sign.

"Another client of mine gave me a hug after I gave her a check," he said.

I stood up and reluctantly hugged him, but I felt as though he was using the fact that I was so compliant, since my brain injury. I asked for copies of the depositions of Drs. Cucumb and Andreassen, plus a copy of the last part of my own deposition that he had refused to give me previously.

"I'm too tired to look for these depositions," he said.

I stood up and started to go through the boxes with the records on my case. He finally came over and gave me the depositions of Drs. Krell, and Deavila. He said he would send me the others later.

In March, I called Mr. Bukinshaw to ask for a copy of the Judgment from Judge Mozz, the one stating that brain damage was considered a physical injury.

"I don't have it anymore," Bukinshaw told me.
Later on, I called to inquire about the depositions of Drs. Cucumb and Andreassen, but was told that the partner's law firm had all the files on the case. Mr. Bukinshaw said he was personally not involved anymore. He told me to call Mr. O'Looney and Mr. White to obtain the depositions.

When I called O'Looney asking about the depositions and the explanation of the papers I had signed when he gave me the check, he talked with me. I had sent him a registered letter requesting this information and asked him if he had received the letter.

"I've been in trial, but I'll answer your letter. I'm very busy and I don't know when I'll have time to do it," he said.

"Could you please send me a copy and an explanation of the papers I signed?" I asked.

"I'll try, but you knew what you were signing," O'Looney said.

"No I did not. I was not even allowed to read the papers," I responded.

"You're a very smart lady," he said. "I don't see what the problem is. You're very smart."

"All I'm asking you is to tell me what it was that you made me sign . . . otherwise, you said you would return the check to Orange Health Insurance. Do I have to contact the defendant's lawyer (Orange Health Insurance) to tell him that what I signed was illegal?

"No. No. I'll see you and explain them to you," he said.

I never received an answer or another appointment from my attorneys. No one would return my calls. Because O'Looney's office continued to ignore my requests, even though I sent a second registered letter, I wrote to the defense attorney asking for a copy of the last volume of my deposition, and for the deposition of Dr. Ray Cucumb. The defense attorney informed me that Dr. Cucumb had never been deposed, despite having been subpoenaed.

White and O'Looney never answered my letter until the defendant's lawyer was contacted by me. I still don't understand the paperwork that O'Looney had me sign. It was never explained. Therefore, it's my belief that this papers are not legal.

These lawyers unjustly and illegally settled my case, against my wishes, forbidding me to seek legal action against Dr. Ray Cucumb for his sexual abuse. I believe these lawyers were illegally influenced by Dr. Cucumb for money, so Cucumb could avoid legal action by the Medical Board of California.

After the lawsuit, I sought psychological treatment. I felt that I had been mentally and psychologically abused by my own lawyers and I didn't know how to deal with it. I felt sorry for the medical care providers that treated me and had not gotten paid by the insurer. Moreover, my lawyers really didn't care.

My psychologist recommended that I speak with a friend of hers, Damien Russe, attorney from Encino, California, which I did. Mr. Russe told me that Mr. Bukinshaw had been put in jail for 15 years. Shocked, I asked, "Are you sure? What did he do to be put in jail?"

"He created false lawsuits for many millions of dollars against health insurance companies and he finally got arrested," he explained.

"You are telling me that my attorney is a criminal?"

"That is why this jerk acted like he did."

"It was in the State Bar Magazine a while ago," he said.

"Let me call the State Bar for you, but I'm sure that Mr. Bukinshaw had been put in jail."

He confirmed it with the State Bar.

"He and his partners all protected each other. They didn't care about my health or my lawsuit. I can't believe it. How come people like this are allowed to practice law?"

Mr. Russe assured me that Mr. Bukinshaw would never be able to practice law again. This was the end of his profession.

Many of us often wonder why there are so many problems in

our beautiful country, the United States of America. It seems our legal, medical and political systems including the health institutions and insurance companies have far too much power and can get away with using us. There seems no end to it, no limit.

Through my experience I learned that each of us must take responsibility for our own lives. We must learn about our medical problems and take control of our own health as best we can. I learned the hard way, through many errors. I will never again trust insurance providers to do what they say and I will always be wary of attorneys. I realize how naive I was to blindly trust the professional individuals I thought were helping me recover from the devastating results of my accident.

I have decided to live each day, no matter what my limitations are. I exercise regularly and strive to find new dreams to make my life more fulfilling. I appreciate the time I have with my husband and my daughter, and am grateful for the inspiration of my deceased father. Though it is sometimes very difficult, as in the experience I had with my attorneys. I try to laugh when things don't work out well. Instead of asking, "Why?" I now say, "What am I going to do next?"

Chapter 19 - Today

On December 27th, 1995, it will be 13 years since this tragic accident took place. As we all know, every day we create new parts in our life, and life brings us new scenarios that we don't really expect to face.

I was informed that lawyer Anson likes being a Superior Court Judge very much.

Lawyer Gaines's goal today is to also be named Judge. I was told he does the most he can in his profession to reach that political point.

Lawyer Bukinshaw is still in jail for violating Rico law (*Federal and state laws designed to investigate, control, and prosecute organized crime)* and for three counts of mail fraud. He was given the maximum sentence of 16 years in jail, and fined $100,000.

Mr. Koosch, attorney at law, is still practicing in Torrance, California, with a new staff member; his son. This law firm operates with maximum professionalism. Any client that needs legal services, would be extremely happy with the integrity and dignity of Lawyer Koosch.

My best friends, Dustin and Arlene, have since died. *God has obtained a luminous man of integrity . . . Dustin.* The *Angel* that was always there for me . . . has now left. I have physically lost my greatest American lady friend, Arlene Devitt. *She was a woman of dignity.* I miss them terribly.

Inside of six years I physically lost my husband, John, Dr. Omar Lahlou, Dustin and Arlene. They were between the ages of 38 and 43. They were all healthier than me. They were living *Angels* there to help Véronique and me. God decided that he needed them. It was their time to go.

Today, my life continues . . .

Simone's husband divorced her after those scenarios that she played in my life following my accident, I was told, and she is no longer an airline stewardess.

I was also informed that Cécile's boyfriend, Arman, whom she had been with for eight years, also left her. In addition, she lost her business in bankruptcy.

After the good and bad scenarios that René played in my life after my accident, he acted in wrongdoing at the hospital where he worked as a registered nurse. He has been dismissed and his license has been revoked.

My daughter, Véronique, is growing as a beautiful adult, and she is very happy and is determined to succeed in all her goals. She is considering a career in law enforcement.

Today my life continues . . .

Nine years ago I had my last back surgery. I'm now facing a new one. Since February 1995, when I felt that I reinjured the lumbar region of my back, I've had pain in my right buttock, right leg, knee and foot. In addition, I had to fight back one more time in court to be referred to Dr. Phillip, orthopedist, from the Cedars-Sinai Medical Center. I lost in the Small Claims Court, and won my case against the insurer. The insurer paid for all of my medical expenses, plus court fees.

My health insurer is MedPlan HMO. Therefore, I have to have a primary physician that is supposed to refer me to a specialist in his group plan if needed. It doesn't matter if they're competent or not, it doesn't matter if they know my medical condition or not. This group of IPA physicians, after reading a referral form that my primary physician sent them, decides if I should see a specialist or continue to take prescribed medication . . . and they dislike very much referring a patient to a specialist. *(When they refer patients to specialists, they lose money that they would otherwise be entitled to at the end of the year.)* So, imagine, the referral form that was sent to them was full of mistakes. This group refused to let me see a specialist even though I seriously needed to see one. Furthermore, I was not allowed to communicate with them in any possible way. The IPA would decide if and when I should see a specialist.

In February 1995, I went to see my primary physician, Dr. Guay, and described the back pain I was having. I wanted to know what could be done to relieve me of it. He examined me and decided to prescribe pain pills and said that it should help. "I am afraid to have my vertebrae diffused," I told Dr. Guay.

I started to take Naprosyn (500 mg) for pain in February of 1995. The following month, March of 1995, I had a trip already organized to go to Rosarito Beach Hotel in Mexico. When I came back from my trip, my lumbar back pain was much more severe. Therefore, I saw my primary physician and told him that I would like to be referred to Dr. Phillip, the orthopedist who took care of me after my accident, or Dr. Edmund, a neurologist. These are both doctors in the Los Angeles area who are the most familiar with my medical condition. In addition, I asked Dr. Guay to send me for an MRI, Myelogram, Cat Scan or a Polytone test. He gave me one refill of Naprosyn (500 mg), and told me that he understood the severity of my back injuries and he would refer me to Dr. Phillip if the pain persisted. I took these pills as prescribed, and the pain wouldn't go away. I continued to see my primary physician a few times a month, in April and May, always for the same back pain that created so many problems to the right side of my body, and I was losing the reflex of my right leg. He would continue to pre-scribe pain pills. In April I got another refill for Naprosyn (500 mg). At the beginning of May, he prescribed Motrin (800 mg). It was a pain killer, I was told. Then, because the pain persisted, he prescribed Darvocet-N (100mg). In addition to these pills, I used the Tens Unit on my back all night long.The medications and use of the Tens Unit did not bring me any relief. The next visit I had with Dr. Guay, I asked him again to refer me to Dr. Phillip, or any other orthopedist. I couldn't continue my life in pain. His answer was that the IPA refused to send me to see a specialist. I had to take pain pills first.

After four months of taking pain pills, I just couldn't play the HMO, IPA and primary physician's game anymore. I came home and called my insurer. I was informed that my primary physician, Dr. Guay, had all authority to refer his patients to whomever he wanted. That was his decision, the member representative, Marsha, had said.

I went back to see Dr. Guay, told him what the insurer had told me, and showed him the written note that I had of my telephone conversation with the insurer's employee, Marsha.

"Would you please call her . . . here is the phone number," I said. "She will tell you what she told me."

"What this person said is wrong," he responded. But, I will let you see Dr. Phillip. I know a lady at the IPA that will give me an authorization number."

May 5th, 1995, Dr. Guay suggested that I get an X-ray for *bilateral sacroiliac joints.* One of his secretaries called the X-ray office and made an appointment for me immediately. I went there and got it taken care of. Later on, I was informed by my primary physician that I didn't have any problem in that joint according to the radiologist.

I continued to see Dr. Guay every week for that serious back pain. He talked with my insurer quite a few times without much result. During every medical visit, I asked my physician to authorize me to have an MRI. His answer was always the same. "You must take the pain killers first, Odette. The IPA will refuse otherwise."

June 8th, during my visit with my primary physician, Dr. Guay verbally authorized me to see my orthopedist, and advised me to bring the bilateral sacroiliac joints X-rays with me to show them to Dr. Phillip. "Let me call the X-ray office, and go pick it up," he said. "It is important that your doctor look at these X-rays."

June 12th, 1995, I had an appointment with an HMO orthopedist. After examining me, he suggested that I get an MRI done to the lumbar region of my vertebrae. I asked him if he could call Dr. Guay to get his authorization. His secretary called my primary physician, and his employee in charge of referrals refused to allow us to speak with my primary physician, saying that it would take two to three weeks before getting an authorization number after she asked for it, and Dr. Guay could not do anything about it.

June 22nd, 1995, I finally received an authorization number to have an MRI test done. I called immediately to the X-ray office to arrange an appointment, and the employee in charge of this type of test said that she didn't have any idea when I could get the MRI done. I called the same office again both on June 23rd and 26th, only to be told that they still could not give me an appointment for the MRI. I was told they didn't have any idea when it could be scheduled. It might be one month or longer, the receptionist said.

That same day, I called my orthopedist at the Cedars-Sinai Medical Center to make an appointment. I was able to see him the day after.

On the morning of June 27th, 1995, I called Dr. Edmund regarding an MRI that would show if the fusion was broken. Dr. Edmund said, "Go get a MRI at Medical Diagnosis Imaging."

I responded, "The IPA and my primary physician don't want me to have this test. I have been asking Dr. Guay since February to send me for an MRI and he has refused, telling me that the IPA will not send me for an MRI."

"Call Dr. Guay and ask him to call me. I will be in my Thousand Oaks office all day."

After this telephone conversation, I called back to my primary physician and gave his secretary the message. Then, I left to see Dr. Phillip. During my time there, the orthopedist looked at the X-rays, performed a physical exam on the lumbar region of my back and legs. Then he said, "These X-rays do not show what is wrong. I believe that you have an overgrowth of bone. We don't see this often. In this hospital I think there are two cases of overgrowth of bone. But I think that the pain you have is from an overgrowth of bone. We might have to perform an exploratory surgery to see what the problem is."

I was not sure what he was talking about. I asked, "Are you telling me that I have bone growing on my vertebrae?"

"Yes," he said, "The pain seems to be from an overgrowth of bone. To be sure, we would have to do an exploratory surgery."

He then called Dr. Guay, explained my medical condition, and suggested that I get an epidural steroid injection, and recommended that I undergo an MRI with a gadopentetate dimeglumine injection, before discussing surgery. Following their conversation, he gave me a cortisone shot, then he prescribed Prednisone (5 mg). Furthermore, he wanted to see me in two weeks. On my way home I stopped at the drug store and got the prescription filled.

I arrived home, and I had two identical phone calls on my answering machine. One from my primary physician's secretary, telling me to go to Medical Diagnosis Imaging (MDI) on June 30th to have an MRI done at eleven o'clock, and the second call was from the insurer's X-ray office telling me exactly the same thing. The orthopedist and my neurologist who had taken care of me for over nine years, were once again in charge of my medical case and would help me to get adequate medical care.

I started taking Prednisone (5 mg) every day as prescribed. It was the first time in five months that I was finally able to have relief from pain. I was now able to sleep on my back, right side of my body and on my stomach.

When I was at MDI Medical Center, I learned that my health insurance didn't have any type of MRI equipment, Cat Scan equipment, and so on, and that this HMO health insurer that I belonged to was forced to send their patients to other medical clinics for these tests to be taken.

It made me realize why this incompetent, negligent HMO company had refused for so long to allow me to have this test as prescribed by Dr. Phillip and one of their own orthopedists.

On July 11th, I went back to see Dr. Phillip after being authorized by my primary physician. I showed him the MRI result like Dr. Guay wanted me to do. But before performing any type of surgery like the HMO orthopedist wanted to do immediately for a disc herniation, Dr. Phillip repeated what he had told me on June 27th. I should have a nerve root block under X-ray control *(the purpose of the block is to put a drug directly where the nerve is being pinched. If the nerve is being pinched as it exits the spine, the radiologist must put the needle under X-ray control at the exiting point to inject either a local anesthetic or a cortisone drug)* because that might save me from surgery. Before sending me to the Cedars-Sinai Medical Center, he asked his assistant, Lynn, to call my primary physician. She called Dr. Guay's office and told his secretary what Dr. Phillip wanted to do. Brenda said that the HMO refused to pay for my visits with my orthopedist and he should not see me because it was not covered by the insurer. Therefore, I left the office of Dr. Phillip without receiving any medical care.

July 17th, 1995, I called my primary physician regarding the tremendous pain in my back and leg. I left a message with his secretary, asking him to call me back. He never returned my phone call.

It is important not to forget that during these six months of chaos with the HMO insurer, the IPA, and my primary physician, I saw two orthopedists from the HMO plan. The first one, after examining my back and talking about my previous back surgeries, said, "Even though I have been an orthopedist for 15 years, I don't want to work on a damaged back like yours." The second one wanted me to have an MRI done, but the HMO refused.

July 20th, 1995, Dr. Guay prescribed more pain pills. This time

Vicodin ES. I took one pill and got extremely sick. I was sure this time that I would die. David entered our bedroom and saw me in terrible condition. He went to our office and looked in the *Family Guide to Prescription Drugs.* He came back into the master bedroom and read to me special warnings about this medication. *Use caution in taking Vicodin ES if you have a head injury. The narcotics tend to increase the pressure of the fluid within the skull, which may be exaggerated by head injuries. Side effects of narcotics can interfere in the treatment of patients with head injuries.* That was exactly my case. We just couldn't believe that my physician had prescribed these pain killer pills for me.

The day after, I went to my primary physician and showed him what the Prescription Drugs book said about these pills. I told him, "Before prescribing pain pills, you should call my neurologist, Dr. Edmund, and ask him what you can prescribe for me because of my brain injury. Dr. Edmund is a very competent neurologist and he knows my medical condition."

Dr. Guay left me in the examination room. A while later he came back and said, "Take this prescription. It won't create any problem with your brain injury."

I asked him, "Are you sure that these pills won't create a problem?"

"I just called Dr. Edmund, and he suggested that prescription," he said.

I also asked him to authorize me to see Dr. Phillip one more time. Which he did. At the end of the month, I saw my physician again for the same pain, and I told him that I would see Dr. Phillip as he had authorized me, and I would like to have an authorization number.

July 21st, 1995, the second HMO orthopedist prescribed that I get an epidural steroid injection for the lumbar part of my back. I was sent to an anesthesiologist that specialized in that field, and the insurer agreed for me to have this treatment. I visited him and had an epidural steroid injection in my vertebrae. But, because the physician did not know the severity of my lower lumbar spine condition, it turned out to be a waste of time and energy, because it created crucial pain.

The MRI films showed damage to the base of my spine referred to as lumbar 3 and lumbar 4 (L3-L4). The second HMO orthopedist of the group I belong to looked at these films, and said, "I'll do your surgery next week. You have a disc herniation at L3-L4 level. We won't remove everything, just a part of it."

I thanked him and said, "I am going to see Dr. Phillip at the Cedars-Sinai Medical Center to show him these films. If I need surgery, I will have it done by him."

"If he can't do your surgery, come back, and I will do it for you," he said.

August 22nd, 1995, I received a letter from my insurer infoming me of the denial for authorization to see Dr. Phillip. According to my HMO Group, Dr. Phillip was not a contractor provider. This shows how wrong they were, because he was a contractor provider. I was able to prove it by giving them his identification number.

I was so upset to see the way our medical system functions, that I checked everyone I could before deciding to take legal action. I called at my primary physician and asked them to fax me every referral authorization request form that was sent to the IPA since February 1995. I thought that if these referral forms that were sent to the IPA weren't filled out correctly, they would refuse to send me to see a specialist. Susan, from Dr. Guay's office, faxed me the forms that I requested. I couldn't believe all of the mistakes that were on them. I decided to take my primary physician and the person from his office responsible for the referral form to the Small Claims Court like I was advised by my lawyer.

Three days later, I saw Dr. Guay at his office and I elicited the court process against him and one of his employees.

October 6th, 1995, I showed up in court as plaintiff, with my daughter to help me. The defendant, Dr. Guay, and Beverly, his employee, were present. I was suing for Dr. Phillip's fee to see me and the court fees.

Even though my lawyer had told me that the primary physician and the IPA are not responsible, but the insurer is entirely at fault, I wanted to sue them to prove a point. These private health insurance companies should not be allowed to abuse and neglect their patients.

The following week after I went to court, the insurer's employee, Andrea, called me to say that they decided to pay for my appointment with Dr. Phillip. I told her that I had already gone to court with my physician.

She said, "If you lose in court, don't worry. Send me the verdict, and we will pay you."

I told her," I want to be paid for the court fee also."
There was no problem, said Andrea. She also sent it to me in writing. Shortly thereafter, I received the verdict. I lost in court, but won against the insurer. I was reimbursed for all my expenses by the insurer.

In our culture, we should not allow HMO health insurance companies to abuse patients, and physicians to be in conflict of interest. Physicians that jeopardize our health and life because they belong to an HMO group should be suspended by the Medical Association.

It is quite disgusting to realize that in a country like the United States of America, citizens have to fight constantly to get adequate medical services. And, so many Americans cannot even afford to get medical care.

If I had not sued my physician and his employee, I would have lost everything. Now, I feel that I won . . . because I'm getting the medical care from an orthopedist that knows my medical condition very well, and is qualified to give first class attention to his patients. Let me tell you that he is not an HMO physician. He would never accept to be at this low medical level. HMO insurance companies in this country take away professionalism from our physicians. Physicians who have integrity would never approve to be part of an HMO insurer group. How low can our physicians be to play games with their patients' health? There is no human way physicians can take good care of their patients when they have to fight constantly with HMO private health insurers; even though they are in that situation because they choose to.

Today, my life continues . . .

Today, I have a new primary physician, and I am allowed to see Dr. Phillip. I received authorization for nerve root block under X-ray control like we had been asking for the previous June. I went to the Cedars-Sinai Medical Center pain management group and got this prescription taken care of. This treatment didn't help me, therefore, my only chance to recuperate was through surgery. I called Dr. Phillip's assistant, Lynn, and told her I would like to have a myelogram done to the lumbar part of my back to make sure that we knew what we would be facing before operating. I simply didn't want to be paralyzed. This is what scared me the most. The following day, I received a telephone call from Lynn, and she told me that the HMO was refusing to authorize a myelogram. "Would you please tell them that they had better authorize this medical test, otherwise I will be forced to take legal action," I told her. Late afternoon, a few days later, Lynn called me back telling me that the HMO had given her an authorization number for a myelogram and a Cat Scan.

December 18th, 1995, my husband, my daughter, and Carmen *(a family friend)* accompanied me to the Cedars-Sinai Medical Center for my exploratory surgery. I was sent to a pre-operating room to be prepared for surgery. I told the nurse in charge that I needed to speak to Dr. Phillip. I didn't want anything to take place before talking to him. This distinguished white haired, blue eyed, orthopedist, wearing a green uniform and a white mask attached around his neck, entered the pre-operating room, and said, "You asked to see me, Odette." "Dr. Phillip, I am very afraid to paralyze. If there is work that needs to be done around the sciatic nerve, would you please not touch it. I am afraid to paralyze . . . there is no chance to take . . . make sure that no one touches the sciatic nerve." I elicited my deepest fear to my physician.

"Don't worry! Everything will be find. I have to go now; and don't worry," my surgeon said. That was the end of it. My walking future was in his hands. But, I had one more demand to make before the anesthesiologist injected the needle into my right arm to put me to sleep.

"God and dad, please help me. I want to wake up and be able to walk. David and Véronique need me. Make sure that I wake up and I am able to walk."

During the evening, David and Véronique told me that it was a surgery that took five hours to complete.

The following day, I was waiting desperately to see the ortho- pedist. I was so anxious to know what he had done to my lower back. I knew only one thing; I didn't have any pain in my right leg and foot. It took me eleven months to arrive at this point where I was finally free of pain.

December 19th, Dr. Phillip entered my hospital room with a smile on his face, looking very happy and proud. The first thing he said was, "You made history. We have never seen a back like yours. *You had an overgrowth of bone from the fusion.* We have never seen that before. You made history! Your fusion is solid from L4 to the sacrum, at least on the right side." I asked him, "What was creating the pain?"

"We did root decompression from branches of the sciatic nerve at three places, a complete hemilaminectomy was performed, and disc herniation at the L3 level."

He had been informed that I had not taken any pain pills or any other type of medication since the surgery.

"You can be released tomorrow if you want to," he said.

I wasn't emotionally or physically ready to leave. I was released two and half days after the surgery. That was my Christmas gift from God, my Dad, and the people that were praying for me in Canada and the United States of America, *being alive and not pa- ralyze*d.

Currently, I'm back walking with my friends and trying to regain my physical capacity.

I still find life beautiful to live and share with other people. I learned so much psychologically, intellectually, mentally and fi- nancially from these scenarios of the past thirteen years of my second life.

It doesn't matter how much or what type of pain I endured, I succeeded in raising my daughter and giving her beautiful values of life.

No matter what, I am so grateful for what I have. If we are true believers, it is easy to realize that God doesn't give us more than we can handle.

Today, my life continues.

About the Author Now

This is the true story of a woman who fell the distance of a sixty story building . . . and lived to tell about it.

On December 27th, 1982, while walking in the snow in the San Bernardino mountains, Odette Marie B. Kuhlman-Fischer and her husband, John O. Kuhlman, fell down the mountainside. The fall killed her husband and severely injured the entire right side of her body. This is her story . . . . of the long and frustrating struggle to recovery and her battle for justice.

Odette Marie Fischer and I currently reside in Los Angeles, California with our daughter, Véronique. Despite her many injuries and battles, she is buoyant, fiery, and entertaining. Nothing stops her from enjoying life. She wakes in the morning with a smile on her face, a sparkle in her eye and french songs on her lips!

David E. Fischer

Bourget Publishing of California,
welcomes your comments.
Please send letters to
Odds Against Survival / 'gaining insight'
Post Office Box 1028,
Agoura Hills, California 91376 - 1028

Order Form

Fax Orders: Bourget Publishing of California, P.O. Box 1028,
Agoura Hills, California 91376-1028 USA
Fax # 1 (818) 991-0612
Telephone Orders: 1 (818) 706-1623

Please send the following books. I understand that I may return
any book for a full refund...for any reason, no questions asked.

____

____

____

Please add my name to the Bourget Publishing of California so that
I may receive more information on book publishing.

Company Name:_____________________________________

Name:____

Address:____

City:_________________________State:________________

Zip________

Sales tax:

Please add 7.75% for books and 75 cents for each additional book.
(Surface shipping may take three to four weeks)
Air Mail: $3.50 per book

Payment:

Cash, Check, Cashier Check or Money Order

call and order now